FILM AS ART

FILM
AS
ART

Rudolf Arnheim

UNIVERSITY OF CALIFORNIA PRESS

1971 Berkeley, Los Angeles, London

UNIVERSITY OF CALIFORNIA PRESS
Berkeley and Los Angeles, California

UNIVERSITY OF CALIFORNIA PRESS, LTD.
London, England

© 1957, by
The Regents of the University of California

Eighth printing, 1971
ISBN: 0-520-00035-8

Library of Congress Catalog Card Number: 57-10496

Designed by Rita Carroll

Printed in the United States of America

1968

FOREWORD

An unexpectedly brisk second wind has kept this book moving after it was reshaped and revived a dozen years ago. The sustained demand, especially on the part of the ever-increasing number of young film friends, must mean that the thesis of the book stands the test of time. In fact, these days whenever some scenes of a new or old film exert the spell of art, they do so by the direct impact of moving shapes and sounds, not by talk. The indirectness of language, so magically evocative in its own domain of literature and drama, makes words fade into meaningless noise when they are forced to compete on an equal footing with the immediacy of visual and auditory action. Television proves daily how revealing a small gesture, caught from life, can be for the eye of the beholder and, on the other hand, how tediously absurd is the endless exposure of talking human bodies. Speech, wisely subordinated, supplements, explains, and deepens the image; but the image continues to rule the screen, and to explore its properties remains a topical task.

Confirmed again, it seems to me, is the observation that the film derives its principal strength from the realism of the photographic medium. How hopelessly artificial looks the puppet play of pretentious mystery-making in the Swedish manner or the slick window display of tangled nudes in the French way! And how promptly are such contrivances infused with momentary life, almost against their will, by the spontaneity of an unspoiled actor or landscape.

The authentic realism of the film image has recently produced its most striking artistic results not so much by exposing the cruelties of the physical world, as it did in the twenties and forties; rather, it has given a new tangible truth to the inner workings of the mind, the fantasies and reminiscences, the domain over time and space. Perhaps this fills a vacuum left by the other visual arts. Painters and sculptors, as they used to be called, seem to have reacted to the subjectivity and detachment of the modern mind by retreating to the making of objects that betray their human origin as little as possible. The film, for its part, has responded by making us walk more confidently on the precarious ground of imagination.

As its styles and applications change, the film medium reveals itself more and more clearly. Its basic, invariant character was discernible in the old examples and continues to be recognized in the inventions of filmmakers today.

Rudolf Arnheim
Cambridge, Massachusetts

CONTENTS

1957

A PERSONAL NOTE

The writings that are here collected date back to the thirties. The first part of the book is taken from *Film,* written and published under the title *Film als Kunst* in Germany, shortly before Hitler came to power. An English translation by L. M. Sieveking and Ian F. D. Morrow was published in 1933 in London by Faber and Faber, who graciously gave permission for this partial republication. The book has been out of print for many years. The articles written in 1933 and 1934 in Rome for the projected *Enciclopedia del Cinema* are printed here for the first time. I have translated them from the German manuscripts. "A Forecast of Television" was published in *Intercine,* a periodical of the International Institute for Educational Film, in February 1935. "A New Laocoön" is translated from the original Italian text, which appeared in 1938 in *Bianco e Nero,* a monthly connected with the State film school in Rome.

To go back to my writings about film means more than retracing my steps. It means reopening a closed chapter. The reader of this book will find that film is, to me, a unique experiment in the visual arts which took place in the first three decades of this century. In its pure state it survives in the private efforts of a few courageous individuals; and occasional flares, reminis-

1

cent of a distinguished past, light up the mass production of the film industry, which permitted the new medium to become a comfortable technique for popular storytelling. Correspondingly, the author of this book has changed from a monomaniac, who sank into his studies of the motion picture whatever he had learned about psychology and art, to a stray customer, who gratefully enjoys—a few times a year—the screen performances of intelligent artists and for the rest refers to the film in his lectures and writings when a contribution of the animated photograph serves to illustrate a particular point. Thus in a recent book, *Art and Visual Perception,* film and filmlike effects carry much of the chapter on motion.

Compared with the broader aspects of artistic vision, which have absorbed my attention lately, film seems a limited subject. Yet what attracted the young student in the twenties was not only the new, phantastic, inquisitive, aggressive, and sentimental play of moving shadows in itself, but also a critical challenge to certain principles of theory. It frequently happens that a guiding theme, whose development will occupy a man's later life, takes shape around his twentieth year. At about that time I started to make copious notes on what I called *Materialtheorie.* It was a theory meant to show that artistic and scientific descriptions of reality are cast in molds that derive not so much from the subject matter itself as from the properties of the medium—or *Material*—employed. I was impressed by the geometrically and numerically simple forms, by the regularity and symmetry found in early cosmologies as well as in Bohr's atomic model, in philosophical systems, and in the art of primitives and children. At the time, my teachers Max Wertheimer and Wolfgang Köhler were laying the theoretical and practical foundations of gestalt theory at the Psychological Institute of the University of Berlin, and I found myself fastening on to what may be called a Kantian turn of the new doctrine, according to which even the most elementary processes of vision do not produce mechanical recordings of the outer world but organize the sensory raw material creatively according to principles of simplicity, regularity, and balance, which govern the receptor mechanism.

This discovery of the gestalt school fitted the notion that the work of art, too, is not simply an imitation or selective duplication of reality but a translation of observed characteristics into the forms of a given medium. Now obviously, when art was thus asserted to be an equivalent rather than a derivative, photography and film represented a test case. If a mechanical reproduction of reality, made by machine, could be art, then the theory was wrong. In other words, it was the precarious encounter of reality and art that teased me into action. I undertook to show in detail how the very properties that make photography and film fall short of perfect reproduction can act as the necessary molds of an artistic medium. The simplicity of this thesis and the obstinate consistency of its demonstration explain, I believe, why a quarter of a century after the publication of *Film* the book is—still and again—consulted, asked for, and stolen from libraries.

The first part of *Film*, which develops the thesis, has worn reasonably well and is reproduced here practically complete under the headings "Film and Reality" and "The Making of a Film." I have omitted much of the rest: some of the chapters tangled with tasks for which respectable techniques are now available, such as my sketchy "content analysis" of the standard movie ideology; others dealt with temporary questions—for example, the early fumblings of the sound film—now mercifully forgotten. The translation of what is left has been revised sentence by sentence, and many a puzzling statement attributed to me in the earlier edition is now restored to its intended meaning.

More of a problem than the barrier of language, however, was the distance in time. I found myself dealing with my writings as though with the work of a favorite student: pleased to have engendered a kindred mind, a little worried perhaps at his precocious possession of thoughts I cherished as my own, more ruthless in condemnation and correction than when less involved, and yet as meticulous as affection demands. This means that in editing and translating the material I have tried to preserve the meaning rather than the word, the argument rather than the sentence; I have eliminated details that sounded redundant or untenable, built qualifications into brash assertions, tightened loose reasoning. But nothing substantial is changed. I have not added anything, not tried to bring things up to date either with regard to my own thinking or to the technological progress and the film production of the intervening years. Some technical references will sound quaint to the expert of today. No film cited is less than twenty years old, and most of them are much older. I do not consider this a defect. Nothing of what has happened in the meantime seems to me new enough in principle to require inclusion in a book that is not a chronicle but a theory of film, except perhaps the remarkable blossoming of the "abstract" film—the beginnings of what someday will be the great art of painting in motion. As to my own position, I still believe what I believed then, and I find that my predictions have been borne out. The talking film is still a hybrid medium, which lives from whatever fragments of the visual language were salvageable and from the beauty of the creatures, things, and thoughts it reproduces; the color film, incapable of controlling its multidimensional instrument, has never gone beyond tasteful "color schemes"; the stereoscopic film is still unrealizable technically, and in its recent substitutes has increased the realism of the performance to the extent of requiring first-aid stations in the theaters without exploiting the new resources artistically; the wide screen, finally, has gone a long way toward destroying the last pretenses of a meaningfully organized image. The critics, to be sure, still find occasion for the highest praise, but then, as a matter of survival, their standards shift with the times. In the meantime, television viewers are noticing that live performances are better than "canned" ones. This sounds like the knell of justice for the illusionists: he who vies with nature deserves to lose!

A word should be said about the Italian writings collected in this book. The International Institute for Educational Film, established in Rome by the League of Nations, reached beyond the scope that was defined by its name. When I joined the staff in 1933, its enterprising director, Dr. Luciano de Feo, had begun to collect from experts all over the world material for an encyclopedia which was to cover in two large volumes the historical, artistic, social, technical, educational, and juridical aspects of the motion picture. The work, which was to be published by Ulrico Hoepli in Milan, was in page proof when Italy left the League of Nations in 1938 and all large-scale activity of the institute ceased. As one of the editors of the encyclopedia I wrote many articles, of which two are selected here. The longer piece, "The Thoughts That Made the Picture Move," discusses the many quaint technical devices that finally led to the inventions of Lumière and Edison; but instead of treating them in their historical order, as has been done more completely by others, it considers them as the stages of a thought process that took place collectively in many brains.

"A New Laocoön," last in this collection, was also last to be written. Exasperatingly quixotic though the piece may appear even in this somewhat shortened English version, it raises the basic aesthetic question of how various media can be combined in one work of art. By putting film in the context of the other arts, it also broadens the basis of operation and leads on to problems that lie beyond the covers of this book.

Something more hopeful and more helpful might have been written, the reader may feel, if there had been less insistence on "art" and more gratitude for useful and enjoyable evenings spent in the movie theater. Indeed there would be little justification for an indictment that charged violation of this or that aesthetic code. The issue is a more real one. Shape and color, sound and words are the means by which man defines the nature and intention of his life. In a functioning culture, his ideas reverberate from his buildings, statues, songs, and plays. But a population constantly exposed to chaotic sights and sounds is gravely handicapped in finding its way. When the eyes and ears are prevented from perceiving meaningful order, they can only react to the brutal signals of immediate satisfaction.

This book, then, is a book of standards. It will help preserve the remnants of the attempts to reflect our century in undisturbed animated images. It will transmit some of the principles derived from that experience to the new generation of devotees, who are crowding the showings of the film societies, struggling as private film makers, experimenting with amateur cameras, trying to smuggle the goods into advertising and television, or haunting the mansions of the motion-picture industry. Trying to preserve the standards is worth while. In the thirties, the Italian students who are now the directors and script-writers of many of the admired neorealistic films were hamstrung by Fascism. They found an outlet in analyzing the classics of film art and the texts of film theory with the fanatic devotion of cloistered medieval scholars. Their imagination and keen observation could hardly have borne such remarkable fruit, were it not for the erudition and the sense of quality acquired in those years. Their works are full of good quotations.

These films and those of other talented artists, however, are also beset by the impurities that are so amply diagnosed in this book. It is the business of the theorist to inspect the tools and to ask that they be cleaner. At the same time he is darkly aware of what the reckless practice of the arts has done to his standards in the past and will do to them in the future. Having delivered his admonition, he secretly puts some trust in the messy shrewdness that for so long has been the hope of the human condition.

1933

SELECTIONS ADAPTED FROM *FILM*

1   Film and Reality

Film resembles painting, music, literature, and the dance in this respect—it is a medium that may, but need not, be used to produce artistic results. Colored picture post cards, for instance, are not art and are not intended to be. Neither are a military march, a true confessions story, or a strip tease. And the movies are not necessarily film art.

There are still many educated people who stoutly deny the possibility that film might be art. They say, in effect: "Film cannot be art, for it does nothing but reproduce reality mechanically." Those who defend this point of view are reasoning from the analogy of painting. In painting, the way from reality to the picture lies via the artist's eye and nervous system, his hand and, finally, the brush that puts strokes on canvas. The process is not mechanical as that of photography, in which the light rays reflected from the object are collected by a system of lenses and are then directed onto a sensitive plate where they produce chemical changes. Does this state of affairs justify our denying photography and film a place in the temple of the Muses?

It is worth while to refute thoroughly and systematically the charge that photography and film are only mechanical reproductions and that they therefore have no connection with art—for this is an excellent method of getting to understand the nature of film art.

With this end in view, the basic elements of the film medium will be examined separately and compared with the corresponding characteristics of what we perceive "in reality." It will be seen how fundamentally different the two kinds of image are; and that it is just these differences that provide film with its artistic resources. We shall thus come at the same time to understand the working principles of film art.

THE PROJECTION OF SOLIDS UPON A PLANE SURFACE

Let us consider the visual reality of some definite object such as a cube. If this cube is standing on a table in front of me, its position determines whether I can realize its shape properly. If I see, for example, merely the four sides of a square, I have no means of knowing that a cube is before me, I see only a square surface. The human eye, and equally the photographic lens, acts from a particular position and from there can take in only such portions of the field of vision as are not hidden by things in front. As the cube is now placed, five of its faces are screened by the sixth, and therefore this last only is visible. But since this face might equally well conceal something quite different—since it might be the base of a pyramid or one side of a sheet of paper, for instance—our view of the cube has not been selected characteristically.

We have, therefore, already established one important principle: If I wish to photograph a cube, it is not enough for me to bring the object within range of my camera. It is rather a question of my position relative to the object, or of where I place it. The aspect chosen above gives very little information as to the shape of the cube. One, however, that reveals three surfaces of the cube and their relation to one another, shows enough to make it fairly unmistakable what the object is supposed to be. Since our field of vision is full of solid objects, but our eye (like the camera) sees this field from only one station point at any given moment, and since the eye can perceive the rays of light that are reflected from the object only by projecting them onto a plane surface—the retina—the reproduction of even a perfectly simple object is not a mechanical process but can be set about well or badly.

The second aspect gives a much truer picture of the cube than the first. The reason for this is that the second shows more than the first—three faces instead of only one. As a rule, however, truth does not depend on quantity. If it were merely a matter of finding which aspect shows the greatest amount of surface, the best point of view could be arrived at by purely mechanical calculation. There is no formula to help one choose the most characteristic aspect: it is a question of feeling. Whether a particular person is "more himself" in profile than full face, whether the palm or the outside of the hand is more expressive, whether a particular mountain is better taken from the north or the west cannot be ascertained mathematically—they are matters of delicate sensibility.

Thus, as a preliminary, people who contemptuously refer to the camera as an automatic recording machine must be made to realize that even in the simplest photographic reproduction of a perfectly simple object, a feeling for its nature is required which is quite beyond any mechanical operation. We shall see later, by the way, that in artistic photography and film, those aspects that best show the characteristics of a particular object are not by any means always chosen; others are often selected deliberately for the sake of achieving specific effects.

REDUCTION OF DEPTH

How do our eyes succeed in giving us three-dimensional impressions even though the flat retinae can receive only two-dimensional images? Depth perception relies mainly on the distance between the two eyes, which makes for two slightly different images. The fusion of these two pictures into one image gives the three-dimensional impression. As is well known, the same principle is used in the stereoscope, for which two photographs are taken at once, about the same distance apart as the human eyes. This process cannot be used for film without recourse to awkward devices, such as colored spectacles, when more than one person is to watch the projection. For a single spectator it would be easy to make a stereoscopic film. It would only mean taking two simultaneous shots of the same incident a couple of inches apart and then showing one of them to each eye. For display to a larger number of spectators, however, the problem of stereoscopic film has not yet been solved satisfactorily—and hence the sense of depth in film pictures is extraordinarily small. The movement of people or objects from front to back makes a certain depth evident—but it is only necessary to glance into a stereoscope, which makes everything stand out most realistically, to recognize how flat the film picture is. This is another example of the fundamental difference between visual reality and film.

The effect of film is neither absolutely two-dimensional nor absolutely three-dimensional, but something between. Film pictures are at once plane and solid. In Ruttmann's film *Berlin* there is a scene of two subway trains passing each other in opposite directions. The shot is taken looking down from above onto the two trains. Anyone watching this scene realizes, first of all, that one train is coming toward him and the other going away from him (three-dimensional image). He will then also see that one is moving from the lower margin of the screen toward the upper and the other from the upper toward the lower (plane image). This second impression results from the projection of the three-dimensional movement onto the screen surface, which, of course, gives different directions of motion.

The obliteration of the three-dimensional impression has as a second result a stronger accentuation of perspective overlapping. In real life or in a stereoscope, overlapping is accepted as due merely to the accidental arrangement of objects, but very marked cuts result from superimpositions in a plane image. If a man is holding up a newspaper so that one corner comes across his face, this corner seems almost to have been cut out of his face, so sharp are the edges. Moreover, when the three-dimensional impression is lost, other phenomena, known to psychologists as the constancies of size and shape, disappear. Physically, the image thrown onto the retina of the eye by any object in the field of vision diminishes in proportion to the square of the distance. If an object a yard distant is moved away another yard, the area of the image on the retina is diminished to one-quarter of that of the first image. Every photographic plate reacts similarly. Hence in a photograph of someone sitting with his feet stretched out far in front of him the subject comes out with enormous feet and much too small a head. Curiously enough, however, we do not in real life get impressions to accord with the images on the retina. If a man is standing three feet away and another equally tall six feet away, the area of the image of the second does not appear to be only a quarter of that of the first. Nor if a man stretches out his hand toward one does it look disproportionately large. One sees the two men as equal in size and the hand as normal. This phenomenon is known as the constancy of size. It is impossible for most people—excepting those accustomed to drawing and painting, that is, artificially trained—to see according to the image on the retina. This fact, incidentally, is one of the reasons the average person has trouble copying things "correctly." Now an essential for the functioning of the constancy of size is a clear three-dimensional impression; it works excellently in a stereoscope with an ordinary photograph, but hardly at all in a film picture. Thus, in a film picture, if one man is twice as far from the camera as another, the one in front looks very considerably the taller and broader.

It is the same with the constancy of shape. The retinal image of a table top is like the photograph of it; the front edge, being nearer to the spectator, appears much wider than the back; the rectangular surface becomes a trapezoid in the image. As far as the average person is concerned, however, this again does not hold good in practice: he *sees* the surface as rectangular and draws it that way too. Thus the perspective changes taking place in any object that extends in depth are not observed but are compensated unconsciously. That is what is meant by the constancy of form. In a film picture it is hardly operative at all—a table top, especially if it is near the camera, looks very wide in front and very narrow at the back.

These phenomena, as a matter of fact, are due not only to the reduction of three-dimensionality but also to the unreality of the film picture altogether —an unreality due just as much to the absence of color, the delimitation of the screen, and so forth. The result of all this is that sizes and shapes do not appear on the screen in their true proportions but distorted in perspective.

LIGHTING AND THE ABSENCE OF COLOR

It is particularly remarkable that the absence of colors, which one would suppose to be a fundamental divergence from nature, should have been noticed so little before the color film called attention to it. The reduction of all colors to black and white, which does not leave even their brightness values untouched (the reds, for instance, may come too dark or too light, depending on the emulsion), very considerably modifies the picture of the actual world. Yet everyone who goes to see a film accepts the screen world as being true to nature. This is due to the phenomenon of "partial illusion" (see p. 24). The spectator experiences no shock at finding a world in which the sky is the same color as a human face; he accepts shades of gray as the red, white, and blue of the flag; black lips as red; white hair as blond. The leaves on a tree are as dark as a woman's mouth. In other words, not only has a multicolored world been transmuted into a black-and-white world, but in the process all color values have changed their relations to one another: similarities present themselves which do not exist in the natural world; things have the same color which in reality stand either in no direct color connection at all with each other or in quite a different one.

The film picture resembles reality insofar as lighting plays a very important role. Lighting, for instance, helps greatly in making the shape of an object clearly recognizable. (The craters on the surface of the moon are practically invisible at full moon because the sun is perpendicular and no shadows are thrown. The sunlight must come from one side for the outlines of the mountains and the valleys to become visible.) Moreover, the background must be of a brightness value that allows the object to stand out from it sufficiently; it must not be patterned by the light in such a way that it prevents a clear survey of the object by making it appear as though certain portions of the background were part of the object or vice versa.

These rules apply, for example, to the difficult art of photographing works of sculpture. Even when nothing but a "mechanical" reproduction is required, difficulties arise which often puzzle both the sculptor and the photographer. From which side is the statue to be taken? From what distance? Shall it be lighted from the front, from behind, from the right or left side? How these problems are solved determines whether the photograph or film shot turns out anything like the real object or whether it looks like something totally different.

DELIMITATION OF THE IMAGE AND DISTANCE FROM THE OBJECT

Our visual field is limited. Sight is strongest at the center of the retina, clearness of vision decreases toward the edges, and, finally, there is a definite boundary to the range of vision due to the structure of the organ. Thus, if the eyes are fixed upon a particular point, we survey a limited expanse. This fact is, however, of little practical importance. Most people are quite unconscious of it, for the reason that our eyes and heads are mobile and we continually exercise this power, so that the limitation of our range of vision never obtrudes itself. For this reason, if for no other, it is utterly false for certain theorists, and some practitioners, of the motion picture to assert that the circumscribed picture on the screen is an image of our circumscribed view in real life. That is poor psychology. The limitations of a film picture and the limitations of sight cannot be compared because in the actual range of human vision the limitation simply does not exist. The field of vision is in practice unlimited and infinite. A whole room may be taken as a continuous field of vision, although our eyes cannot survey this room from a single position, for while we are looking at anything our gaze is not fixed but moving. Because our head and eyes move we visualize the entire room as an unbroken whole.

It is otherwise with the film or photograph. For the purpose of this argument we are considering a single shot taken with a fixed camera. We shall discuss traveling and panorama shots later. (Even these aids in no sense replace the natural range of vision nor are they intended to do so.) The limitations of the picture are felt immediately. The pictured space is visible to a certain extent, but then comes the edge which cuts off what lies beyond. It is a mistake to deplore this restriction as a drawback. I shall show later that on the contrary it is just such restrictions which give film its right to be called an art.

This restriction (though also the lack of any sense of the force of gravity, see p. 32) explains why it is often very difficult to reproduce intelligibly in a photograph the spatial orientation of the scene depicted. If, for example, the slope of a mountain is photographed from below, or a flight of steps from above, the finished picture surprisingly will often give no impression of height or depth. To represent an ascent or descent by purely visual means is difficult unless the level ground can somehow be shown as a frame of reference. Similarly there must be standards of comparison to show the size of anything. To show the height of trees or of a building, for instance, human figures may be introduced beside them. A man in real life looks all round him when he is walking; and even supposing he is going up a mountain path with his eyes fixed on the ground at his feet, he still has a sense of the general lie of the surrounding country in his mind. This perception comes to him chiefly because his muscles and his sense of balance tell him at every instant exactly in what relation his body stands to the horizontal. Hence he can continually assess correctly the visual impression of the slanting surface. In contrast to such a man is one who is looking at a photograph or screen picture. He must depend upon what his eyes tell him without any assistance from the rest of his body. Moreover, he has only that part of the visual situation which is included within the confines of the picture to help him get his bearings.

The range of the picture is related to the distance of the camera from the object. The smaller the section of real life to be brought into the picture, the nearer the camera must be to the object, and the larger the object in question comes out in the picture—and vice versa. If a whole group of people is to be photographed, the camera must be placed several yards away. If only a single hand is to be shown, the camera must be very close, otherwise other objects besides the hand will appear in the picture. By this means the hand comes out enormously large and extends over the whole screen. Thus the camera, like a man who can move freely, is able to look at an object from close to or from a distance—a self-evident truth that must be mentioned inasmuch as from it is derived an important artistic device. (Variations of range and size can also be obtained by lenses of different focal lengths. The effects are similar but involve no change of the distance from the object and, therefore, no change of perspective.)

How large an object appears on the screen depends partly on the distance at which the camera was placed from it, but partly also on how much the picture is enlarged when the finished film is projected. The degree of enlargement depends on the lens of the projection machine and on the size of the theater. A film may be shown in whatever size is preferred—as small as the pictures in a child's magic lantern or gigantic as in a movie palace. There is, however, an optimum relationship between the size of the picture and its distance from the spectators. In a motion-picture theater the spectator sits relatively far away from the screen. Hence the projection must be large. But those watching pictures in a living room are quite close to the screen and therefore the projection may be much smaller. Nevertheless, the range of sizes used in practice is wider than is altogether desirable. In large theaters the projection is larger than in small ones. The spectators in the front rows naturally see a much larger picture than those in the back rows. It is, however, by no means a matter of indifference how large the picture appears to the spectator. The photography is designed for projection of a particular relative size. Thus in a large projection, or when the spectator is near the picture, movements appear more rapid than in a small one, since in the former case a larger area has to be covered than in the latter. A movement which seems hurried and confused in a large picture may be perfectly right and normal in a smaller one. The relative size of the projection, moreover, determines how clearly the details in the picture are visible to the spectator; and there is obviously a great difference between seeing a man so clearly that one can count the dots on his tie, and being able to recognize him only vaguely—more especially since, as has been pointed out, the size in which the object is to appear is used by the film director to obtain a definite artistic effect. Thus by the spectator's sitting too near or too far away a most disagreeable and obvious misrepresentation of what the artist intended may arise. Up to the present it is impossible to show a film to a large audience so that each member of it sees tł e picture in its right dimensions. After all, spectators must, as far as possible, be placed one behind the other; because when the rows of seats extend too far sideways, those sitting at the ends will see the picture distorted—and that is even worse.

ABSENCE OF THE SPACE-TIME CONTINUUM

In real life every experience or chain of experiences is enacted for every observer in an uninterrupted spatial and temporal sequence. I may, for example, see two people talking together in a room. I am standing fifteen feet away from them. I can alter the distance between us; but this alteration is not made abruptly. I cannot suddenly be only five feet away; I must move through the intervening space. I can leave the room; but I cannot suddenly be in the street. In order to reach the street I must go out of the room, through the door, down the stairs. And similarly with time. I cannot suddenly see what these two people will be doing ten minutes later. These ten minutes must first pass in their entirety. There are no jerks in time or space in real life. Time and space are continuous.

Not so in film. The period of time that is being photographed may be interrupted at any point. One scene may be immediately followed by another that takes place at a totally different time. And the continuity of space may be broken in the same manner. A moment ago I may have been standing a hundred yards away from a house. Suddenly I am close in front of it. I may have been in Sydney a few moments ago. Immediately afterward I can be in Boston. I have only to join the two strips together. To be sure, in practice this freedom is usually restricted in that the subject of the film is an account of some action, and a certain logical unity of time and space must be observed into which the various scenes are fitted. For time especially there are definite rules which must be obeyed.

Within any one film sequence, scenes follow each other in their order of time—unless some digression is introduced as, for example, in recounting earlier adventures, dreams, or memories. Within such a flashback, again, time passes naturally, but the action occurs outside the framework of the main story and need not even stand in any precise time relationship ("before" or "after") to it. Within individual scenes the succession of separate events implies a corresponding sequence of time. If, for example, a "long shot" of a man raising a revolver and firing it is shown, the raising and firing cannot be shown again afterward as a close-up. To do so would be to make a sequence of events that were in fact simultaneous.

That things are happening simultaneously is of course most simply indicated by showing the events in one and the same picture. If I see someone writing at a table in the foreground and someone else in the back playing the piano, the situation is self-explanatory as far as time is concerned. This method is, nevertheless, often avoided for artistic reasons and the situation composed of separate shots.

If two sequences of the action are to be understood as occurring at the same time they may simply be shown one after the other, in which case, however, it must be obvious from the content that simultaneity is intended. The most primitive way of giving this information in a silent film is by printed titles. ("While Elise was hovering between life and death, Edward was boarding the liner at San Francisco.") Or something of this sort: A horse race has been announced to begin at 3:40. The scene is a room full of people who are interested in the race. Someone pulls out a watch and shows the hands pointing to 3:40. Next scene—the racecourse with the horses starting. Events occurring simultaneously may also be shown by cutting up the various scenes and alternating the sections so that the progress of the different events is shown by turns.

Within the individual scenes the time continuum must never be disturbed. Not only must things that occur simultaneously not be shown one after the other, but no time must be omitted. If a man is going from the door to the window, the action must be shown in its entirety; the middle part, for example, must not be suppressed and the spectator left to see the man starting from the door and then with a jerk arriving at the window. This gives the feeling of a violent break in the action, unless something else is inserted so that the intervening time is otherwise occupied. Time may be dropped in the course of a scene only to produce a deliberately comic effect—as, for instance, when Charlie Chaplin enters a pawnbroker's shop and emerges instantly without his overcoat. Since to show complete incidents would frequently be dull and inartistic, because superfluous, the course of the action is sometimes interrupted by parts of scenes taking place simultaneously somewhere else. In this way it can be arranged to show only those moments of each event which are necessary for the action without patching together things that are incoherent in time. Apart from this, each scene in a good film must be so well planned in the scenario that everything necessary, and only what is necessary, takes place within the shortest space of time.

Although the time continuum within any individual scene must remain uninterrupted, the time relationship between scenes that occur at different places is undefined in principle so that it may be impossible to tell whether the second scene takes place before, during, or after the first. This is very clearly shown in many educational films where there is no connection in time but only in subject. As, for example: ". . . not only rabbits but also lions may be tamed." First picture—performing rabbits. Within this scene the continuity of time must be observed. Second picture—lion taming. Here too the continuity of time must not be broken. These two scenes, however, have no sort of time connection. The lion taming may go on before, during, or after the performance with the rabbits. In other words, the time connection is of no consequence and therefore does not exist. Similar situations arise occasionally in narrative films.

If sequences are meant to follow each other in time, the content of the film must make this relationship clear, precisely as in the case of simultaneity; because the fact that two sequences follow each other on the screen does not indicate in itself that they should be understood as following each other in time.

Film can take far greater liberties with space and time, however, than the theater can. To be sure, in the theater it is also permissible to have one scene occur at quite a different time and place from the preceding scene. But scenes with a realistic continuity of place and time are very long-drawn-out and allow of no break. Any change is indicated by a definite interruption—the curtain is lowered or the stage darkened. It might, nevertheless, be imagined that an audience would find it disturbing to see so many disconnected events on one and the same stage. That this is not so is due to a very curious fact: the illusion given by a play (or film) is only partial. Within any particular scene value is laid on naturalism. The characters must talk as people do in real life, a servant like a servant, a duke like a duke. (But even here we have this restriction: the servant and the duke are to talk clearly and sufficiently loudly, that is really, too clearly and loudly.) An ancient Roman lamp must not be put to light a modern drawing room nor a telephone by

Desdemona's bed. Yet the room has only three walls —the fourth, the one that should intervene between the stage and the audience, is missing. Any audience would laugh if a piece of scenery fell down and revealed the wall of the room to be nothing but painted canvas, or if the crack of a shot were heard some seconds before the revolver was fired. But every audience takes it for granted that on the stage a room has only three walls. This deviation from reality is accepted because the technique of the stage demands it. That is to say, the illusion is only partial.

The stage is, so to speak, in two different but intersecting realms. It reproduces nature, but only a part of nature—separate in time and space from the actual time and space of the "house," where the audience is located. At the same time, the stage is a showcase, an exhibit, the scene of action. Hence it comes into the domain of the fictitious. The component of illusion is relatively strong in theater because an actual space (the stage) and an actual passage of time are given. The component of illusion is very slight when we are looking at a picture—for example, a photograph lying on the table in front of us. The photograph, like the stage, represents a particular place and a particular time (a moment of time), but it does not do this as is done in the theater with the aid of an actual space and an actual passage of time. The surface of the picture *signifies* a pictured space; and that is so much of an abstraction that the picture surface in no way gives us the illusion of actual space.

Film—the animated image—comes midway between the theater and the still picture. It presents space, and it does it not as on the stage with the help of real space, but, as in an ordinary photograph, with a flat surface. In spite of this, the impression of space is for various reasons not so weak as in a still photograph. A certain illusion of depth holds the spectator. Again, in contrast with the photograph, time passes during the showing of a film as it does on the stage. This passage of time can be utilized to portray an actual event, but is, nevertheless, not so rigid that it cannot be interrupted by breaks in time without the spectator feeling that these breaks do violence to it. The truth is that the film retains something of the nature of a flat, two-dimensional picture. Pictures may be displayed for as long or short a time as one pleases, and they can be shown next to one another even if they depict totally different periods in time.

Thus film, like the theater, provides a partial illusion. Up to a certain degree it gives the impression of real life. This component is all the stronger since in contrast to the theater the film can actually portray real —that is, not simulated—life in real surroundings. On the other hand, it partakes strongly of the nature of a picture in a way that the stage never can. By the absence of colors, of three-dimensional depth, by being sharply limited by the margins on the screen, and so forth, film is most satisfactorily denuded of its realism. It is always at one and the same time a flat picture post card and the scene of a living action.

From this arises the artistic justification for what is called montage. It was pointed out above that film, which records real situations on strips of celluloid that may be joined together, has the power of placing in juxtaposition things that have no connection at all in real time and space. This power was, however, primarily a purely mechanical one. One might expect the spectator to be overcome by a physical discomfort akin to seasickness when watching a film that had been composed of different shots. For example: In Scene 1 a man is discovered ringing the front doorbell of a house. Immediately following appears a totally different view—the interior of the house with a maid coming to answer the door. Thus the spectator has been jerked violently through the closed door. The maid opens the door and sees the visitor. Suddenly the viewpoint changes again and we are looking at the maid through the visitor's eyes—another breakneck change within the fraction of a second. Then a woman appears in the background of the foyer and in the next moment we have bridged the distance separating us from her, and we are close beside her.

It might be supposed that this lightning juggling with space would be most unpleasing. Yet everyone who goes to the movies knows that actually there is no sense of discomfort, but that a scene such as the one just described can be watched with perfect ease. How can this be explained? We have been talking as though the sequence had actually taken place. But it is not real and—which is of the greatest importance— the spectators have not the (complete) illusion of its reality. For, as has already been said, the illusion is only partial and film gives simultaneously the effect of an actual happening and of a picture.

A result of the "pictureness" of film is, then, that a sequence of scenes that are diverse in time and space is not felt as arbitrary. One looks at them as calmly as one would at a collection of picture post cards. Just as it does not disturb us in the least to find different places and different moments in time registered in such pictures, so it does not seem awkward in a film. If at one moment we see a long shot of a woman at the back of a room, and the next we see a close-up of her face, we simply feel that we have "turned over a page" and are looking at a fresh picture. If film photographs gave a very strong spatial impression, montage probably would be impossible. It is the partial unreality of the film picture that makes it possible.

Whereas the theater stage differs from real life only in that the fourth wall is missing, the setting of the action changes, and the people talk in theatrical language, the film deviates much more profoundly. The position of the spectator is continually changing since we must consider him located at the station point of the camera. A spectator in the theater is always at the same distance from the stage. At the movies the spectator seems to be jumping about from one place to another; he watches from a distance, from close to, from above, through a window, from the right side, from the left; but actually this description, as has been said, is altogether misleading, because it treats the situation as physically real. Instead, pictures taken from the most various angles follow one another, and although the camera position had to be changed continually when they were taken, the spectator is not obliged to duplicate all this commotion.

Many people who are accustomed to clear thinking will feel that this theory of "partial illusion" is vague and equivocal. Is not the very essence of illusion that it should be complete? Is it possible, when one is surrounded by one's own friends and sitting in a chair at home in New York, to imagine oneself in Paris? Can one believe that one is looking at a room when a moment ago a street was there? Yes; one can. According to an outdated psychology that is still deeply rooted in popular thought, an illusion can be strong only if it is complete in every detail. But everyone knows that a clumsy childish scribble of a human face consisting of two dots, a comma, and a dash may be full of expression and depict anger, amusement, or fear. The impression is strong, though the representation is anything but complete. The reason it suffices is that in real life we by no means grasp every detail. If we observe the expression on somebody's face, we are far from being able to say whether he had blue eyes or brown, whether he was wearing a hat or not, and so on. That is to say, in real life we are satisfied to take in essentials; they give us all that we need to know. Hence if these essentials are reproduced we are content and obtain a complete impression that is all the more artistic for being so strongly concentrated. Similarly, in film or theater, so long as the essentials of any event are shown, the illusion takes place. So long as the people on the screen behave like human beings and have human experiences, it is not necessary for us to have them before us as substantial living beings nor to see them occupy actual space— they are real enough as they are. Thus we can perceive objects and events as living and at the same time imaginary, as real objects and as simple patterns of light on the projection screen; and it is this fact that makes film art possible.

ABSENCE OF THE NONVISUAL WORLD OF THE SENSES

Our eyes are not a mechanism functioning independently of the rest of the body. They work in constant coöperation with the other sense organs. Hence surprising phenomena result if the eyes are asked to convey ideas unaided by the other senses. Thus, for example, it is well known that a feeling of giddiness is produced by watching a film that has been taken with the camera traveling very rapidly. This giddiness is caused by the eyes participating in a different world from that indicated by the kinesthetic reactions of the body, which is at rest. The eyes act as if the body as a whole were moving; whereas the other senses, including that of equilibrium, report that it is at rest.

Our sense of equilibrium when we are watching a film is dependent on what the eyes report and does not as in real life receive kinesthetic stimulation. Hence certain parallels which are sometimes drawn between the functioning of the human eye and the camera— for instance, the comparison between the mobility of the eyes and that of the camera—are false. If I turn my eyes or my head, the field of vision is altered. Perhaps a moment ago I was looking at the door; now I am looking at the bookcase; then at the dining-room table, then at the window. This panorama, however, does not pass before my eyes and give the impression that the various objects are moving. Instead I realize that the room is stationary as usual, but that the direction of my gaze is changing, and that that is why I see other parts of the motionless room. This is not the case in film. If the camera was rotated while the picture was being shot, the bookcase, table, window, and door will proceed across the screen when the picture is projected; it is they which are moving. For since the camera is not a part of the spectator's body like his head and his eyes, he cannot tell that it has been turned. He can see the objects on the screen being displaced and at first is led to assume that they are in motion. In Jacques Feyder's *Les Nouveaux Messieurs*, for example, there is a scene in which the camera passes rapidly along a long wall covered with posters. The result is that the wall seems to move past the camera. If the scene that has been photographed is very simple to understand, if it is easy to get one's bearings in it, the spectator corrects this impression more or less rapidly. If, for instance, the camera is first directed toward a man's legs and if it then pans slowly up toward his head, the spectator knows very well that the man did not float feet first past a stationary camera. Film directors, however, often turn or shift the camera for taking pictures that are not so easy to grasp, and then a sensation of drifting supervenes which may be unintentional and may easily make the audience feel dizzy. This difference between the movements of the eyes and those of the camera is increased because the film picture has, as was said above, a fixed limit whereas the field of vision of our eyes is practically unbounded. Fresh objects are continually appearing within the frame of the picture and then disappearing again, but for the eyes there is an unbroken space-continuum through which the gaze wanders at will.

Thus there is relativity of movement in film. Since there are no bodily sensations to indicate whether the camera was at rest or in motion, and if in motion at what speed or in what direction, the camera's position is, for want of other evidence, presumed to be fixed. Hence if something moves in the picture this motion is at first seen as a movement of the thing itself and not as the result of a movement of the camera gliding past a stationary object. In the extreme case this leads to the direction of motion being reversed. If, for example, a moving car is filmed from a second one which is overtaking the first, the finished picture will show a car apparently traveling backward. It is, however, possible to make clear which movement is relative and which absolute by the nature and behavior of the objects shown in the picture. If it is obvious from the picture that the camera was standing on a moving car, that is, if parts of this car are seen in the picture, and, contrary to the landscape, they stay in the same place in the picture, the car will be perceived as moving and the surrounding landscape as stationary.

There is also a relativization of spatial coördinates—above, below, and so forth. To this are partly due the phenomena we described above in the section on the "Delimitation of the Image." A photograph of a slanting surface may not give an appearance of slope because there is no sensation of gravity to help the spectator realize "up and down." It is impossible to feel whether the camera was standing straight or was placed at an angle. Therefore, as long as there is nothing to indicate the contrary, the projection plane is perceived as vertical. If the camera is held over a bed to show from above the head of a man lying in it, the impression may easily be given that the man is sitting upright and that the pillow is perpendicular. The screen is vertical, although since the camera was turned downward it actually represents a horizontal surface. This effect can be avoided only by showing enough of the surroundings in the picture to give the spectator his bearings.

As regards the other senses: No one who went unprejudiced to watch a silent film missed the noises which would have been heard if the same events had been taking place in real life. No one missed the sound of walking feet, nor the rustling of leaves, nor the ticking of a clock. The lack of such sounds (speech, of course, is also one of them) was hardly ever apparent, although they would have been missed with a desperate shock in real life. People took the silence of the movies for granted because they never quite lost the feeling that what they saw was after all only pictures. This feeling alone, however, would not be sufficient to prevent the lack of sound being felt as an unpleasant violation of the illusion. That this did not happen is again connected with what was explained above: that in order to get a full impression it is not necessary for it to be complete in the naturalistic sense. All kinds of things may be left out which would be present in real life, so long as what is shown contains the essentials. Only after one has known talkies is the lack of sound conspicuous in a silent film. But that proves nothing and is not an argument against the potentialities of silent film, even since the introduction of sound.

It is much the same with the sense of smell. There may be people who if they see a Roman Catholic service on the screen imagine that they can smell incense; but no one will miss the stimulus. Sensations of smell, equilibrium, or touch are, of course, never conveyed in a film through direct stimuli, but are suggested indirectly through sight. Thence arises the important rule that it is improper to make films of occurrences whose central features cannot be expressed visually. Of course a revolver shot might occur as the central point of a silent film; a clever director could afford to dispense with the actual noise of the shot. It is enough for the spectator to see the revolver being fired and possibly to see the wounded man fall. In Josef von Sternberg's *The Docks of New York* a shot is very cleverly made visible by the sudden rising of a flock of scared birds.

2   *The Making of a Film*

It has been shown above that the images we receive of the physical world differ from those on the movie screen. This was done in order to refute the assertion that film is nothing but the feeble mechanical reproduction of real life. The analysis has furnished us with the data from which we can hope to derive now the principles of film art.

By its very nature, of course, the motion picture tends to satisfy the desire for faithful reports about curious, characteristic, exciting things going on in this world of ours. The first sensation provided by film in its early music-hall days was to depict everyday things in a lifelike fashion on the screen. People were greatly thrilled by the sight of a locomotive approaching at top speed or the emperor in person riding down *Unter den Linden.* In those days, the pleasure given by film derived almost entirely from the subject matter. A film art developed only gradually when the movie makers began consciously or unconsciously to cultivate the peculiar possibilities of cinematographic technique and to apply them toward the creation of artistic productions. To what extent the use of these means of expression affects the large audiences remains a moot question. Certainly box-office success depends even now much more on what is shown than on whether it is shown artistically.

The film producer himself is influenced by the strong resemblance of his photographic material to reality. As distinguished from the tools of the sculptor and the painter, which by themselves produce nothing resembling nature, the camera starts to turn and a likeness of the real world results mechanically. There is serious danger that the film maker will rest content with such shapeless reproduction. In order that the film artist may create a work of art it is important that he consciously stress the peculiarities of his medium. This, however, should be done in such a manner that the character of the objects represented should not thereby be destroyed but rather strengthened, concentrated, and interpreted. Our next task will be to bring examples to show how the various peculiarities of film material can be, and have been, used to achieve artistic effects.

ARTISTIC USE OF PROJECTIONS UPON A PLANE SURFACE

In an earlier section I showed what conditions arise from the fact that in a photographic representation three-dimensional bodies and spaces are projected on a two-dimensional plane, that is, the surface of the picture. It was first demonstrated that an object can be reproduced characteristically or otherwise according to what view of it is chosen. When film art was in its infancy, nobody paid much attention to the subleties of these problems. The camera was stationed well in front of the people to be photographed in order that their faces and movements might be easily seen. If a house was to be shown, the cameraman placed himself straight in front of it at such a distance that nothing would be left out of the picture. It was only gradually that the particular effects that can be achieved by means of perspective projection were realized.

In Chaplin's film *The Immigrant* the opening scene shows a boat rolling horribly and all the passengers being seasick. They stagger to the side of the ship pressing their hands to their mouths. Then comes the first shot of Charlie Chaplin: he is seen hanging over the side with his back to the audience, his head well down, his legs kicking wildly—everyone thinks the poor devil is paying his toll to the sea. Suddenly Charlie pulls himself up, turns round and shows that he has hooked a large fish with his walking stick. The effect of surprise is achieved by making use of the fact that the spectator will be looking at the situation from a certain definite position. The idea underlying the scene is no longer "a man is doing such and such a thing, for example, he is fishing or being sick," but "a man is doing this and that, *and* at the same time the spectator is watching him from a particular station point." The element of surprise exists only when the scene is watched from one particular position. If the scene had been taken from the waterside, the audience would have realized at once that Charlie was not being sick but was fishing; and hence the wrong idea would not have first been implanted. The invention is no longer concerned merely with the subject matter but is cinematographic inasmuch as a definite feature of film technique is being used as a means to secure an effect.

It is in the nature of such a scene that what is happening should not be obvious to the audience. In order to obtain a special effect the artist works exactly contrary to the principle of "the most characteristic view." In Dupont's *Vaudeville* the first appearance of the central character is planned on much the same principle. The convict Jannings is seated opposite the examining magistrate; his face is not yet visible, only his broad back can be seen with a large numeral sewed to his coat. Thus with the help of a pictorial symbol an idea which in itself is abstract, purely intellectual, and unvisual—"This is only one of a crowd, not an individual but simply a number"—is made manifest. In a film planned on more fantastic lines the convict might have been shown without a head and in place of the head a number floating above the trunk—as is sometimes done in caricatures (a businessman's body surmounted by a dollar sign instead of a human head). What is arresting, however, in Dupont's scene is that in order to symbolize the abstract it was not found necessary to interfere with reality. An entirely natural view, justified by the action, was chosen, and the desired effect was obtained purely by taking the shot from a particular angle—an unforced, specific occurrence, the view so chosen and so recorded that it was typical and symbolic.

Thus the conditions under which the picture is taken (in our example, the choice of a particular angle of approach) are not treated as negligible quantities or necessary evils, but are consciously brought into relief as factors contributing to the composition of the picture. The artistic effect is, indeed, achieved precisely by using them. The episode "Conversation between magistrate and convict" in itself is distinguished from the reproduction of this episode by the particular standpoint from which the reproduction was made. It had to be selected definitely out of a hundred visual possibilities. But this very "limitation" yields the artistic opportunity of making the particular pictured event convey an idea.

The present attempt to make a systematic analysis must not be taken as a psychological description of how this scene was invented. In other words, it must not be taken to mean that Dupont's mental process was something like this: "I must have a symbolic representation of a convict as nothing but a number. What method shall I use to produce this effect? Ah! The camera angle . . . let me think . . ." It may have happened the other way around. The director may accidentally have seen the convict from the back and thus have lit on the happy idea. We are here concerned only with analyzing the finished work and studying its effects.

In the Russian films—other people have copied the idea—the domineering forcefulness of a character is often expressed by taking the shot from the worm's-eye view. An iron captain of industry or a general—the camera looks up at him as at a mountain. Here again the fact that the actor has to be taken from some particular point of view is not handled perfunctorily but is consciously exploited: the perspective angle acquires meaning, a virtue is made of necessity.

A twofold effect can be produced by a clever position of the camera. If an artistic impression is to be achieved, this double effect is necessary; and must not only show the subject in characteristic fashion but must at the same time satisfy the spectator's sense of form. To photograph an autocrat from below not only points the effect which the figure is to have upon the audience, but, if cleverly executed, it also results in an arresting play of form. It is unusual—or was until a few years ago—consciously to perceive such a distorted view of the human body. The hugeness of the body, the head—appearing very small because of the foreshortening—far away on top of the figure, the curious displacement of the facial structure (the way the tip of the nose with its two black caverns juts out over the mustache; the chin seen from below)—all this possesses a strong formal interest which need not imply anything with regard to the content. The strangeness and unexpectedness of this view have the effect of a clever *coup d'esprit* ("to get a fresh angle on a thing"), it brings out the unfamiliar in a familiar object. René Clair's film *Entr'acte* contains a picture of a ballet girl dancing on a sheet of glass. The photograph has been taken from below through the glass. As the girl dances, her gauze skirts open and close like the petals of a flower and in the middle of this corolla comes the curious pantomime of the legs. The pleasure derived from so curious a shot is at first purely formal and is divorced from all meaning. It arises solely from the pictorial surprise. If in addition it had some significance, its value would be all the greater. The erotic element of the dance, for instance, might be brought into prominence at will by such a position of the camera.

Camera angles are often chosen solely on account of their formal interest and not for their meaning. A director has perhaps discovered some ingenious viewpoint which he insists on using even though it signifies nothing. In a good film every shot must be contributory to the action. Nevertheless, directors very often allow themselves to be led into violating this principle. They will show two people in conversation; they will take the picture from the level and then suddenly from the ceiling, looking down onto the heads, even though the shift in viewpoint brings out or proves or explains nothing. All that these directors have succeeded in accomplishing is the betrayal of their art.

In Carl Dreyer's beautiful film *The Passion of Joan of Arc* long discussions take place between priests and the Maid. This is an unfruitful theme for the camera. The real interest of these scenes lies in the spoken word. Visually there is little variety to be extracted from the endless confrontations of arguing speakers. The solution of the difficulty is surely to avoid putting scenes like this into a silent film. Carl Dreyer decided otherwise, and mistakenly. He tried to animate these cinematographically uninspiring episodes by variety in form. The camera was most active. It took the Maid's head obliquely from above; then it was aimed diagonally across her chin. It looked up the ecclesiastical judge's nostrils, ran rapidly toward his forehead, took him from the front as he put one question, from the side as he put the next—in short, a bewildering array of magnificent portraits, but lacking in the slightest artistic meaning. This byplay contributes nothing to the spectator's comprehension of the examination of the Maid; on the contrary, the spectator is irrelevantly entertained to prevent his being bored by what should be exciting. Form for form's sake—this is the rock on which many film artists, especially the French, are shipwrecked.

The curious camera angles to be found in many recent films—adopted either with artistic intent or merely for their own sake—were looked upon as malpractices in the early days of photography and film. In those days anyone would have been ashamed to present an audience with an oblique camera angle. What are the reasons for this change?

The fascination of the early films lay in the movement on the screen of objects which exactly resembled their originals in real life and behaved like them down to the minutest detail. This attitude toward film naturally determined the position from which shots were taken. Whatever was to be shown was taken from the angle which most clearly presented it and its movements. The task of the camera was in fact considered to be merely that of catching and registering life. The idea that the manner in which this was done might be of value in itself or do the job of recording information even more efficiently was not yet considered. People were not in those days dealing with film as an art but merely as a medium of recording. "Distortion" was obviously wrong since it was not yet intentional.

Only gradually, and at first probably without conscious intention, the possibility of utilizing the differences between film and real life for the purpose of making formally significant images was realized. What had formerly been ignored or simply accepted was now intelligently developed, displayed, and made into a tool to serve the desire for artistic creation. The object as such was no longer the first consideration. Its place in importance was taken by the pictorial representation of its properties, the making apparent of an inherent idea, and so forth.

Another aspect remains to be touched upon. An unusual camera angle (such as those mentioned above) has still another result apart from characterizing the object in a particular sense and introducing an attractive element of surprise by the unexpected shapes which a familiar object can assume. Pudovkin has said that film strives to lead the spectator beyond the sphere of ordinary human conceptions. For the ordinary person in everyday life, sight is simply a means of finding his bearings in the natural world. Roughly speaking, he sees only so much of the objects surrounding him as is necessary for his purpose. If a man is standing at the counter of a haberdasher's shop, the salesman will presumably pay less attention to the customer's facial expression than to the kind of tie he is wearing (so as to guess his taste) and to the quality of his clothes (so as to know what his requirements are likely to be). But when the same man enters his office his secretary will doubtless pay less attention to his tie than to his facial expression (so as to know what sort of temper he is in). It is a well-known fact that many married couples do not know the color of each other's eyes; that people are ignorant of the very pictures hanging on the walls of their dining rooms; that they do not know what the carpet on their floors is like; and that they have never noticed how their servants are dressed. It is indeed exceptional—apart from persons of aesthetic tastes and training—for anyone suddenly to lose himself in gratuitous contemplation, to watch his neighbor's hands, to examine the telephone for its shape, to observe the play of shadows on the pavement.

In order to understand a work of art, however, it is essential that the spectator's attention should be guided to such qualities of form, that is, that he should abandon himself to a mental attitude which is to some extent unnatural. For example, it is no longer merely a matter of realizing that "there stands a policeman"; but rather of realizing "how he is standing" and to what extent this picture is characteristic of policemen in general. Notice how well the man is selected; what a characteristic movement that one is in comparison with another, more obvious movement; and how the forcefulness of the figure is brought out by the shot being taken from below!

There are also certain artifices by which the spectator may be induced to assume such an attitude. If an ordinary picture of some men in a rowing boat appears on the screen, the spectator will perhaps merely perceive that here is a boat, and nothing further. But if, for example, the camera is suspended high up, so that the spectator sees the boat and the men from above, the result is a view very seldom seen in real life. The interest is thereby diverted from the subject to the form. The spectator notices how strikingly spindle-shaped is the boat and how curiously the bodies of the men swing to and fro. Things that previously remained unnoticed are the more striking because the object itself as a whole appears strange and unusual. The spectator is thus brought to see something familiar as something new. At this moment he becomes capable of true observation. For it is not only that he is now stimulated to notice whether the natural objects have been rendered characteristically or colorlessly, with originality or obviously, but by stimulating the interest through the unusualness of the aspect the objects themselves become more vivid and therefore more capable of effect. In watching a good shot of a horse I shall have a much stronger feeling that "here is an actual horse—a big beast with a satiny skin, and with such and such a smell . . ." That is to say, therefore, not only form but also objective qualities will impose themselves more compellingly. It must, however, be mentioned that if this method is applied unskillfully it leads to the opposite result and may produce a view of the object which makes it quite unrecognizable, or which shows it so much out of character that the effect is not strengthened but lost.

It may be convenient to summarize briefly here what has been said in the above paragraphs:

It is a property of photography that it must represent solids "one-sidedly" as plane pictures. This reduction of the three-dimensional to the two-dimensional is a necessity of which the artist makes a virtue. It is the means by which he achieves the following results:

1) By reproducing the object from an unusual and striking angle, the artist forces the spectator to take a keener interest, which goes beyond mere noticing or

acceptance. The object thus photographed sometimes gains in reality and the impression it makes is livelier and more arresting.

2) The artist, however, does not direct the attention merely toward the object itself, but also to its formal qualities. Stimulated by the provocative unfamiliarity of the aspect, the spectator looks more closely and observes (*a*) how the new perspective shows up all sorts of unexpected shapes in the various parts of the object, and (*b*) how the solid which has been projected onto a plane surface now fills the space as a flat picture with a pleasing arrangement of outlines and shadow masses—thus making a good and harmonious effect. This design is achieved without any distortion or violation of the object, which appears simply as "itself." Hence the striking artistic effect.

3) Guiding the attention to the formal attributes of the object has the further result that the spectator now feels inclined to consider whether the object has been chosen characteristically and whether its behavior is characteristic; in other words, whether it is a representative example of its genus (for example, "a typical official") and whether it moves and reacts in conformity with its species.

4) The novel camera angle, however, serves not only as an alarm and decoy. By showing the object from a particular point of view, it can interpret it, more or less profoundly ("The convict as a number"). Here too, there is a special charm in that to obtain this result the object has in no way been changed or touched up, but has been left exactly as it appears in real life.

The projection of solids upon a plane not only implies that each individual object must be shown from a particular angle, but the relative positions of various bodies, the way they cut into one another, must also be discussed. Physical bodies occupy a position in space; one can walk about amongst them, look at each separately. But if a film camera is placed in a particular spot—the traveling camera will not at present be considered—it sees the objects one behind the other exactly as does the human eye (when the observer is standing still), one object obstructing the view of another. And this limitation again helps the artist to achieve quite special effects. Let us take a notable example:

In Alexander Room's *The Ghost That Never Returns* the following fine scene occurs. A convict has been released from prison. He is seen going away from the audience down a long road between two enormously high stone walls. In a crack in the wall he finds something which he has probably not seen for years—a little flower. The flower serves as the (somewhat banal) symbol of nature and freedom, which he has been obliged to forgo for so long. He picks the flower. Then he suddenly loses his temper, turns about to face the camera, raises his fists threateningly, and shakes them in the direction from which he has been coming. And at this moment the camera leaps to a different position. The direction of view is exactly the same, but the camera is moved a few yards back and now is unexpectedly placed behind the bars of the prison from which the prisoner has just gone out to freedom. The bars now occupy the foreground, very large, covering the whole area of the picture. And through them the same scene appears as before—the road with the ex-convict raising his arms threateningly. This trick on the part of the director is extraordinarily impressive—and most instructive.

The effect is achieved by skillfully making the most of the necessity of deciding upon some one "angle." Setting aside the film camera, and considering only the actual situation, it resolves itself into a barred gate, beyond it a road between two long walls, and a man walking down this road. Any number of camera angles were possible. The camera might have been put at the end of the road. The prison with its barred gate would then have been in the background. The man might have been shown going out through the gate; and the camera might have moved out to freedom with him. A bird's-eye view of the scene might have been presented which would have given a good survey of the whole episode in its surroundings. The angle which the director chose does not give any such general survey. In the first shot the prison is not visible at all. In the second, nothing of the prison is shown but the bars, notwithstanding that the convict has just emerged from the prison, which therefore is a vital element in the scene. It is nevertheless by this very means that the desired effect is achieved. Thus we see again that the artist very often chooses angles which do not at all give the clearest, most obvious, complete prospect of a scene.

Since the film director must decide upon a particular camera angle, he is able to select what objects he will allow to appear in the picture; to conceal what he does not wish to show, or does not wish to show at once (this is done by placing the camera so that the undesired objects are screened by other objects or so that they simply do not come into the picture at all);

to bring into prominence whatever he considers to be important, and very possibly would not of itself show its importance in the scene. In other words, the film director can emphasize objects—make one object conspicuous, hide another that may be disturbing or unimportant, without interfering with the objects themselves or altering them in any way. Moreover, he is able to move objects about so as to emphasize their relation to each other—a relation that may be visually obvious only by placing the camera in some one definite position.

In the first shot in Room's film nothing is seen of the grating, that is, the prison theme does not appear in the picture at all. The spectator sees the convict walking along the road at liberty, freed from the cell. And suddenly the man revolts and the object of his indignation—his imprisonment—is brought into the picture by a brilliant artifice without the necessity for a change of scene. (In many films a picture of the prison or of a cell would have been inset.) The desired effect is simply extracted from the given situation. The grating enters the scene to act as a partner to the liberated convict.

The special excellence of the invention lies not so much in that the prison theme is brought into the picture at all, as in the manner in which it is done. All at once the heavy iron bars of the grating cover the whole screen—the whole view. And these bars are gigantic compared with the man who is playing his part far back in the picture and therefore appears very small. A most convincing symbol of the tremendous power which he is threatening impotently and which still oppresses him.

The film artist who makes a virtue of necessity in taking his shots from a definite angle arranges the objects as he wishes, puts what seems to him important in the foreground, hides other things, suggests relationships. The man and the grating are actually separated by a considerable distance. If the camera had been differently placed, this distance would have been very marked; it might in fact even have proved impossible to get the two objects into the same picture. It is the particular location of the camera that produces the significant connection: man—grating. The grating, which might have remained quite unimpressive if some other angle had been chosen for the shot, and certainly would have remained unnoticed in its symbolic meaning, gains its dominant role from the fact that at first it is not there and then is added to the picture while everything else remains the same. It thereby brings itself into prominence and makes clear that it was not introduced without definite intention. It makes its entrance as if it were one of the actors. Here we see how the film artist quite definitely guides the spectator's attention, gives him directions, indicates the interpretation he is to put upon objects.

It is but seldom and only in the works of great film artists that such a deeply symbolic meaning is produced by such simple means. Usually the significance lies more superficially, sometimes there is none at all. In Pabst's film *The Diary of a Lost Girl* a pharmacist's assistant is seen kissing his employer's daughter. They are standing by the glass door of the shop. The scene is first taken from the interior. The camera is standing in the shop. The shot shows the two kissing each other and beyond them the door which leads out into the street. Then the scene is suddenly shown from another angle—the couple remain in exactly the same position, but the camera is now outside the door and they are seen through the glass. There seems to be no point in this change of the camera's position. It signifies nothing. And things which have no significance have no place in a work of art. The reason for the sequence of the two shots is wholly superficial and decorative. It is attractive to the eye to see the same scene first from within and then from without through the glass panel—a pleasure comparable, perhaps, with that experienced when a composer presents a theme first in the major and then in the minor key. In music such a change of the mode must be justified by the total sequence, so also it must be in a film. Here the device is insufficiently motivated and therefore artistically weak. There might have been sound reason for using these two camera angles, if after the second shot someone were shown looking through the door and watching the scene from outside. This would motivate the sequence through the plot. The viewpoint of the action would have been neatly shifted by means of shot 2 from the interior of the shop to the observer outside, and the change in position of the camera would have been justified artistically. But even then the invention would be somewhat shallow inasmuch as it serves only to give a clever visual interpretation of the action and lacks symbolic depth. (This must not be taken to imply that every shot should be expected to provide the depth of the grating scene in *The Ghost That Never Returns*. On the contrary, the richness of a film composition is served by the varying degrees of profundity underlying the shots.)

In the two examples we have given, a connection is established by means of perspective between two features of a situation—grating and convict in one case, glass door and lovers in the other. This requires transparent objects like the grating and the glass. In other cases, having one object in front of another may serve to conceal the latter. Three examples taken from three dissimilar films will serve to illustrate this device.

The following instance is very much like that chosen from Charlie Chaplin's *The Immigrant* and is in fact taken from one of his shorter films. Charlie has been deserted by his wife because he is a drunkard. He is standing with his back to the camera by a table on which is his wife's photograph. His shoulders are heaving, he is apparently sobbing bitterly. The next moment he turns round. The heaving of his shoulders reveals itself to be the result of his manipulation of a cocktail shaker. Thus the camera angle, which at first presents the scene so that the actual occurrence cannot be seen but only inferred, is once again very skillfully used. The opacity of most physical objects, which makes one body conceal the other from sight, would seem to be a liability for the film artist. This is true, and we shall later see how film directors overcome this obstacle. On the other hand, however, skillful use of this optical fact makes possible a game of hide-and-seek resulting in an unexpected artistic denouement. The revelation is especially effective because there has been no obvious concealment beforehand, no artificial suggestion of secrecy. There is nothing particularly noteworthy about seeing the back view of a man. One feels that one knows exactly what Chaplin is doing: he is sobbing—very naturally, too, since his wife has run away. Hence the spectator feels quite confident that he has grasped the meaning of the scene correctly; the little man then turns round and the surprise "comes off."

In the crime film *The Mysterious Lady* the following scene occurs: Greta Garbo, as a spy, has killed a Russian general in his study. She is in imminent danger of discovery. Outside the door are some soldiers waiting to come in. The general is lying dead in his armchair. The wide back of the armchair is facing the door. Thus the dead man cannot be seen from the door. His forearm is hanging over the arm of the chair and can be seen from the door. The soldiers knock peremptorily. Greta Garbo sits on the arm of the chair and says "Come in!" The camera is now placed so that the spectators see the room exactly as do the soldiers on entering—the wide back of the chair, the general's hand hanging over the arm of the chair, and Greta Garbo sitting beside him with her face turned to the door, that is, toward the audience. The soldiers salute and ask for orders. Greta Garbo turns to the dead man and apparently asks for instructions. She then turns back and communicates these instructions to the soldiers. The soldiers turn right about and march out of the room. The danger has been averted.

In Eisenstein's film *The General Line* a poor peasant woman comes to the farm of a rich man to borrow a horse. The fat kulak is lying on a couch. The woman stands before him and addresses him humbly. He sits up. The camera is then placed behind him. His broad back is seen looming large and heavy in the foreground, finally blotting out entirely the woman who is standing in the background. The whole picture is suddenly filled and dominated by this huge elephantine back. Here again power and arrogance are expressed by means of a clever choice of position. Through being placed close to the camera the back appears particularly large, fat, space-devouring. The peasant woman in the background is very small by contrast. Then an idea is suggested—"power obliterating helplessness"— and the woman disappears from the picture altogether.

In contrast with this is a scene from *The Ghost That Never Returns*, in which one of the prison warders comes into the director's office to deliver a message. The director's high armchair is seen by his desk exactly as the general's armchair in *The Mysterious Lady*, with its back to the audience. At first there seems to be no one sitting in it. But as soon as the warder begins to speak, a little hunchback man peers round the side of the chair—the director's first appearance. Although the effect is unexpected, it is also fairly pointless. This sudden appearance is nothing more than a trick on the part of the film maker; it is not material to the action, and it has not much more significance than if the director happened to fall down off the chandelier for no reason in particular.

A cleverly chosen camera angle may produce a vivid impression not only of an isolated object but of a total setting as well. At the beginning of Jacques Feyder's *Les Nouveaux Messieurs* a rehearsal at the opera is in progress. Such scenes have often been shown before and are usually uninteresting. But here is one among many (some of which manage to be effective by other means) in which vividness is achieved by a clever camera angle. The spectator feels as if he were himself in the very center of the bustle of the stage crowd. How is it done? The camera is placed up in the flies among the machinery and looks down upon the stage. Up above in the dark the silhouettes of two stage hands are seen large in the foreground. They lean over to let a rope down onto the stage. The floor of the stage far below is brightly lit up like the bottom of a shaft. Other stage hands are engaged below in spreading out a carpet, and being so far away give the effect of dwarf figures. The rope dangling down to them is given in great foreshortening. Thus its swinging movement appears curiously cramped and jerky. The abysmal depth, the contrast between the brightly lit stage and the dark flies, the jerking rope, the difference in size between the darkly silhouetted men up above and the others below on the illuminated stage—everything contributes to make the scene startlingly lifelike. One seems to smell the dust and the cold air of the stage.

It has already been pointed out that the need for choosing a particular camera angle, or in other words of showing the various objects one behind another, often gives rise to difficulties. If, for instance, a man is to be shown standing among a group of people and talking to them, it is very hard to find a viewpoint which will give a good survey of the whole scene. Wherever the camera is set up, the backs of the crowd hide the speaker. One way out of the difficulty is to have the camera looking onto the group from above. The speaker is then seen clearly in the center with his listeners gathered round him. A picture taken from such an angle can be found in Arthur Robinson's *The Night after the Betrayal.*

A difficulty which arises a dozen times in every film, and is resolved in as many ways, is a scene between two persons facing each other. It is desired to show clearly the facial expression of both actors. Hence each had best be taken full face. Unfortunately that is precisely what is impossible to do, for when two people are opposite each other only one will be facing the camera, while the other will have his back to it. Both might be given in profile, but this position is seldom interesting, and, moreover, does not give a good view of the faces. Again, one might use montage and show the two figures full face in rapid alternation, thus splitting up the scene one or more times by showing it from the two "best" viewpoints. Or finally, one can risk taking the one player from the back view only. A successful example of this solution is in the Greta Garbo film *A Woman of Affairs* directed by Clarence Brown. A father is giving his son a dressing down. The father is seen in dark silhouette in the foreground with his back to the camera, very large, very near. Sitting farther back, considerably smaller and in bright light, is the son, facing his father and the camera. Hence the father's face is not visible. But what he is saying can be conjectured from his attitude and gestures and, above all, from the play of expression on the son's face. This lecture of which the spectator is thus indirectly apprised "comes over" most effectively and vividly. Here is yet another example of a virtue made of necessity.

Other and quite different solutions to this problem

are found in Jacques Feyder's *Les Nouveaux Messieurs*. Two lovers, for example, are seen in conversation, with their heads close together. Then a close-up is shown in which half the picture is covered by the dark silhouette of the back of the man's head (the camera being placed behind him), and this head partially conceals the woman's full face, of which the remainder is seen in bright light. The bisection is most expressive. One seems to see more by seeing less. Again, the same two people are in the girl's dressing room at the theater. She is sitting in front of the looking glass making herself up. Her face is seen front view in the glass, and beside it that of the man who is tinkering with something in the background and stealing covert glances at her. Thus the spectator sees both at once in full face—although the two are looking at each other—which of course could not have been achieved without the mirror.

Léon Moussinac in his very useful book *Panoramique du Cinéma* (in the chapter on Dupont's *Vaudeville*) points out that the casual succession of clever and appropriate camera angles is an accomplishment of mature film art. Formerly the camera was, as it were, nailed down in front of the actors, while the director tried to place his performers where they would be most clearly seen even at the risk of making the picture somewhat lacking in spontaneity. He says in this connection: "It is particularly important and instructive that in this film the camera has not been considered in a single scene. The camera continually changes its position. The scene, the details, the expressions on the faces of the actors, are taken from the most telling angles. One never sees, for example, several people acting with their faces simultaneously turned to the camera, as is common in the French and in many American films. Jannings' back is as expressive as his face. If we notice a certain mannerism in this respect, one must at least admit that this mannerism serves its purpose admirably. It proves that the most important and fundamental means of expression has been understood by certain film artists—to shoot from any angle so long as it is the most telling. We know that in film the fourth wall of the room in which the action takes place is not simply left out, but that the camera is brought into the actual room and takes part in the story."

It is easy to understand that film directors only very gradually arrived at making effective use of these means. We remarked above that the motion picture derived in the first instance from a desire to record mechanically real events. Not until film began to become an art was the interest moved from mere subject matter to aspects of form. What had hitherto been merely the urge to record certain actual events, now became the aim to represent objects by special means exclusive to film. These means obtrude themselves, show themselves able to do more than simply reproduce the required object; they sharpen it, impose a style upon it, point out special features, make it vivid and decorative. Art begins where mechanical reproduction leaves off, where the conditions of representation serve in some way to mold the object. And the spectator shows himself to be lacking in proper understanding when he is satisfied to notice merely the content: this is the picture of an engine, that of a couple of lovers, and this again of a waiter in a temper.

He must be prepared to turn his attention to the form and to be able to judge *how* the engine, the lovers, the waiter, are depicted.

Every object reproduced in film appears solid and at the same time flat. This fact contributes greatly to the impressive results achieved by the clever shots discussed in the last section. The worm's-eye view of a man appears as such a great distortion of nature because the depth effect is reduced. The same view looked at in a stereoscope seems much less distorted. The contrast between the vast bulk of the trunk and the disproportionately small head is much less forcible when it is perceived as being due to foreshortening. But if there is only slight feeling of space and if the three-dimensional volume of the pictured object is flattened out, a huge body and a little head are seen.

The purely formal qualities of the picture come into prominence only because of the lack of depth. Every good film shot is satisfying in a purely formal sense as a linear composition. The lines are harmoniously disposed with reference to one another as well as to the margins. The distribution of light and shade in the shot is evenly balanced. Only because the spatial effect is so slight, the spectator's attention is drawn to the two-dimensional pattern of lines and shadow masses. These, after all, are actually the components of three-dimensional bodies and become elements of the surface composition only through being projected onto a plane. It has already been mentioned above how the skirt of a dancer seen through a pane of glass seemed to open and close like the petals of a flower. This is an entirely antifunctional effect in that it is not a normally characteristic feature of the skirt as a material object. The curious expansion and contraction of the edge of the skirt results only when it is looked at from one particular viewpoint and then projected upon a flat surface. It would be less noticeable in a stereoscopic view. Only when the feeling of depth is reduced does the up-and-down movement of the skirt give the effect of being an in-and-out movement. It is one of the most important formal qualities of film that every object that is reproduced appears simultaneously in two entirely different frames of reference, namely the two-dimensional and the three-dimensional, and that as one identical object it fulfills two different functions in the two contexts.

The reduction of depth serves, moreover, to emphasize the perspective superposition of objects. In a strongly stereoscopic picture the manner in which these various objects are placed relative to one another does not impose itself any more than it does in real life. The concealing of certain parts of the various objects by others that come in front seems chance and unimportant. Indeed, the position of the camera in a stereoscopic picture seems itself to be a matter of indifference inasmuch as it is obvious that there is a three-dimensional space which may just as easily, and at the next moment probably will, be looked at from another point of view. If, however, the effect of depth is almost negligible, the perspective is conspicuous and compelling. What is visible and what is hidden strike one as being definitely intentional; one is forced to seek for a reason, to be clear in one's own mind as to why the objects are arranged in this particular way and not in some other. There is no leeway between the objects: they are like flat surfaces stuck over one another, and seem almost to lie in the same plane.

Thus the lack of depth brings a very welcome element of unreality into the film picture. Formal qualities, such as the compositional and evocative significance of particular superimpositions, acquire the power to force themselves on the attention of the spectator. A shot like that described above where half of the girl's full face is cut off by the dark silhouette of the man's head, would possess only a fraction of its effectiveness if there were a strong feeling of space. In order to achieve the striking effect it is essential that the division across the face shall not seem accidental but intentional. The two faces must seem to be practically in one plane, with no leeway between them to show that they might easily be moved into different relative positions.

The fact that the lack of depth perception also leads to the almost total disappearance of the phenomena which the psychologist calls the "constancies" of size and form has already been discussed. The film artist takes advantage of their absence to produce remarkable effects. Everyone has seen a railway engine rushing on the scene in a film. It seems to be coming straight at the audience. The effect is most vivid because the dynamic power of the forward-rushing movement is enhanced by another source of dynamics that has no inherent connection with the object itself, that is, with the locomotive, but depends on the position of the spectator, or—in other words—of the camera.

The nearer the engine comes the larger it appears, the dark mass on the screen spreads in every direction at a tremendous pace (a dynamic dilation toward the margins of the screen), and the actual objective movement of the engine is strengthened by this dilation. Thus the apparent alteration in the size of an object which in reality remains the same size enhances its actual activity, and thus helps the film artist to interpret the impact of that activity visually.

The same principle is brought into play when Carl Dreyer in his *The Passion of Joan of Arc* stresses a monk suddenly jumping up excitedly from his seat by placing the camera closely in front of the actor so that through this forward movement his figure grows to an enormous size and occupies the whole screen. Here again the effect of actual dynamic force is intensified by something that is purely of the camera—the sudden rapid extension of the flat projection. If the camera had been placed at a distance of several yards from the monk, the perspective increase in size due to the forward movement would be so slight that it would hardly produce an effect at all.

Pudovkin makes excellent use of perspective alteration in size in *The End of St. Petersburg*. Two starving peasants come to the great city to find work. The vastness of the city compared with the two figures, their personal unimportance and that of their desires in these surroundings, are very strikingly shown in the following shot: In the foreground is a huge dark equestrian statue of a tsar, whose stone hand is imperiously raised. In the background is a wide empty square across which the two peasants are walking, looking like ants. If the depth effect in the shot were great, that is, if the distance between the statue and the two peasants were wholly perceivable, firstly, the difference in size would not be so remarkable but would seem only the natural result of the distance; and, secondly, the two people and the statue would not be so clearly associated and therefore compared with one another. They would obviously lie in quite different planes. In the Pudovkin shot, the spectator sees a spatial situation that he can interpret on the basis of his past experience but that, nevertheless, presents itself to his eyes without the familiar depth effect. Hence two ants are seen to be crawling toward the colossus, and the ants and the colossus are obviously in some kind of connection with one another because their plane of action appears practically identical.

In reality, the two peasants are not much smaller than the statue, and the shot might easily have been taken the reverse way, so that the two would be huge in the foreground and dwarf the stone tsar to a mere accessory in the background. But the significance of Pudovkin's symbolism is to show the two peasants as pathetic, helpless, frightened little creatures, terrified by the size, the stony brutality, the might of the city. The director has cleverly used his power of altering the sizes to make his idea tangible. It has been achieved, again, without any distortion of the actual objects themselves comparable to that which the Egyptians were in the habit of making in their reliefs when they portrayed a victorious king enormously large and his enemies as tiny little figures.

In *The General Line* Eisenstein has in a similar

manner rearranged the natural proportions symbolically. In one scene he wishes to depict a bureaucratic
office setup, in which red tape obstructs any reasonable
conduct of affairs. An official is seen dictating to a
stenographer. The camera is placed immediately in
front of the typewriter in order that the machine may
appear very large. Its roller moves across the screen
like a huge crane; the heads of the typist and the man
dictating appear very small behind it. Then there is a
bookkeeper: the ledger is enormous and the man writing in it quite small. What is first of all an abstract
disparity is made tangible by a corresponding visual
one.

In King Vidor's *The Crowd* the following impressive
scene occurs: A little boy is sitting on the sidewalk
with his friends and is telling them, "My father always
says . . . ," when he sees a crowd in front of his
home—an ambulance—a stretcher being carried into
the house. He runs across full of misgivings. And now
the following shot is shown: The camera is placed
on the second-floor landing, facing down. The front
door is seen below, very small, and from it the staircase leads up widening out in vigorous perspective. Downstairs people are crowding into the house
through the front door, attracted by the news of the
accident. They swarm below like ants. Suddenly the
little boy pushes his way through them. He climbs up
the stairs, slowly, fearfully, and yet burning with
anxiety to learn what has happened. At first he is
very small, then he grows larger, the steps become
wider, the crowd remains below. He comes nearer,
up the wide empty staircase, which grows ever larger

as he approaches the camera, and shows more and more empty space about him. He climbs up—terribly alone—a desolate child, bereft of his father.

The strength of this effect lies in the simplicity and naturalness of the means employed. Nothing is more commonplace than that a staircase gets larger with decreasing distance; but the trite fact, used in this manner, results in a deep, compelling symbolism such as is found in good folk songs.

It must be noted that in the achievement of such an effect much depends on the art of the cameraman. The director or the script-writer may have planned the shot admirably; but if the cameraman does not choose the position for the camera accurately, if he stations it six inches too high or too low, if he puts it exactly in the middle instead of a couple of feet farther over to the left, if he does not choose the lens with the appropriate focal length, the power of the perspective may not emerge in the shot and the idea fall flat. Moreover, the lights must be correctly placed—a little too much light in the background, a spotlight too near the center of the foreground, may radically change the whole shot and destroy the intended effect.

In the early days of the film the director was careful not to have any actor put his hands or his feet too near the camera and thus make them come out disproportionately large. That these apparent alterations in size might be exploited and used to achieve an artistic effect was only realized when the film began to be recognized as an art.

If the artistic capacity of reduced depth has been realized, the efforts of the engineers to create the three-dimensional film will be watched with mixed feelings. In a film which gives a strong illusion of depth the perspective alterations in size have scarcely more effect than they have in real life. Their efficacy as an artistic device will be practically negligible. The two-dimensional relationships, of course, become almost as slight, and the manner in which one object appears behind another in space will be so obvious that the projective as well as any inherent symbolic connections will hardly make themselves felt at all. Engineers are not artists. They therefore do not direct their efforts toward providing the artist with a more effective medium, but toward increasing the naturalness of film pictures. It vexes the engineer that film is so lacking in stereoscopic quality. His ideal is exactly to imitate real life. It provokes him that film should be lacking in colors and sounds; and so he devotes his attention to color photography and sound film. The general, artistically untrained public feels much the same. An audience demands the greatest possible likeness to reality in the movies and it therefore prefers three-dimensional film to flat, colored to black-and-white, talkie to silent. Every step that brings film closer to real life creates a sensation. Each new sensation means full houses. Hence the avid interest of the film industry in these technological developments.

ARTISTIC USE OF LIGHTING AND OF
THE ABSENCE OF COLOR

The question of color is similar to that of depth. When the film artist has to depend on black and white he is offered particularly vivid and impressive effects.

The painter, who does not—as color film does—take colors ready-made from nature but creates them afresh on his palette, is able by suitable choice of tones, by distribution of color masses, and so forth, to get as far away from nature as is necessary to convey his artistic intention. Judging from what we have seen up to now, the colors in a color film are at best naturalistic—and if owing to imperfect technique they are not yet so, this lack of naturalness does not provide the artist with a potentially useful medium of expression.

Whereas the artistic possibilities of color film are still wrapt in obscurity, black-and-white has for many years been a recognized and most effective medium. The reduction of actual color values to a one-dimensional gray series (ranging from pure white to dead black) is a welcome divergence from nature which renders possible the making of significant and decorative pictures by means of light and shade.

The film artist (herein lies the task of the cameraman which is hardly ever properly appreciated) possesses the power to determine very largely what black-and-white values the objects he photographs shall have when projected in the theater. According to how he places his lamps, where he arranges for the shadows to fall, how in out-of-doors work he sets up his camera with regard to the sun, how his screens catch and reflect the light, he can show the same object in the brightest light or in deepest shadow, he can place a light thing in equally light surroundings or let it stand out by contrast against a dark background. This is one of the most important aesthetic possibilities of film. The primitive but always effective symbolism of light versus darkness, white purity versus black evil, the opposition between gloom and radiance, is inexhaustible.

In Sternberg's *The Docks of New York*, for example, the two principal actors of the film are characterized in this way. The white face, the white dress, the white hair of the girl are in visual contrast to the black figure of the ship's stoker. Thus, by a happy, artful congruence, the dramatic interplay of two human minds is made evident through the very elements of visual perception—black-and-white patches moving on the screen. It is obvious that the same effects could not be achieved with color film. In a similar way in Granowsky's *Song of Life* the gripping birth scene in the operating room achieves its deadly silence and harshness chiefly by the pictorial contrast between the long white operating coats, the white sterile sheets, the white cottonwool, and the dark rubber gloves of the doctors with their dark instruments. If this contrast had not been brought out so well by the cameraman, the whole effect of the scene would have been lost.

Consider the face of a blond woman in a film shot: the color of hair and complexion approximate to each other as a curious pale white—even the blue eyes appear whitish; the velvety black bow of the mouth and the sharp dark pencil lines of the eyebrows are in marked contrast. How strange such a face is, how much more intense—because unconventional—is the expression, how much more attention it attracts to itself and to its expression. How much more readily one observes whether the line with which a dense black braid of hair frames a white face is beautiful and suitable. Anyone who has noticed how unreal most film faces appear, how unearthly, how beautiful, how they often give the impression of being not so much a natural phenomenon as an artistic creation—toward which, of course, the art of make-up helps considerably —will get the same pleasure from a good film face as from a good lithograph or woodcut. Anyone who is in the habit of going to film premières knows how painfully pink the faces of the film actors appear in real life when they come on stage and make their bows after the performance. The stylized, expressive giant masks on the screen do not fit beings of flesh and blood; they are visual material, the stuff of which art is made.

The composition of the film image is intelligible and striking chiefly because only black, white, and gray masses, black lines on a white ground, or white lines on a black ground, provide the raw material. A comparison may be made with music, in which articulate statements are possible only because definite pitches of sounds have been arranged in scales, and only these sounds are used in a composition. A sensation of pleasure is aroused by hearing how skillfully these sound values succeed one another. Just as music would be impossible without fixed tones and intervals, so any graphic art—apart from its descriptive and representational function—can have a formal value only if the medium with which the work has been done allows clear definition of shape, brightness, size. This is preëminently the case with black-and-white. All first-class films, especially the good Russian and American ones, show such pronounced black-and-white values —no uncharacteristic confusion of vague, indeterminate tones—that their formal qualities instantly spring to the eye.

The effect of a landscape is almost entirely dependent upon the lighting. There is a famous shot in Walter Ruttmann's symphony of a great city, *Berlin,* in which an empty street in the north of Berlin is shown in the early dawn. The curious mistiness of the morning sky, the veiled darkness of the fronts of the buildings—the apportionment of the gray values, in other words—are what gives this shot its charm. The same street and the same camera angle might result in an utterly feeble and ineffective picture. And obviously these differences can be even more pronounced in the studio where the cameraman has the lights under his control. Ruttmann then has a few men walking down the empty street—workmen on their way to the factory. They are seen in black outline against the gray sky; and these figures in the somewhat lighter street help to emphasize the mystery of the dawn, the strange intermediate state between light and darkness.

One knows the effects that are achieved in crime films by the sudden appearance in a dark room of the spotlight of a pocket lamp that wanders over furniture or perhaps lights up a concealed figure. One knows the wonderful delight that can be given to perceptive eyes by the sensational white of a face that is brightly lit up and in strong relief, the play of clouds scudding across the moon, the shadows of moving leaves on the ground, the flashing of headlights, quivering reflections on water, the shining black of a spot of blood on white skin, the white telegraph wires in Pudovkin's *The End of St. Petersburg* that seem to be cut into the black night sky as with an etcher's needle. But these are delights that are only possible in black-and-white.

If light is cleverly used it also assists in articulating the shape of what is shown. It is only necessary to compare the face of Baranovskaya in one of her Russian films under Pudovkin and in a film made in a foreign studio, such as *Poison Gas,* or *Life's Like That.* It will be noticed that in the Russian film she has very clear-cut features, almost bony, a face vivid and animated by the strong contrasts of light and shade. The same face in the German films appears flat, indistinct, gray, and expressionless. Everything depends on the lighting and the skill with which the shots are taken. Or again, consider Greta Garbo in the German film *The Joyless Street* and in one of her American films. Leaving aside the fact that the German picture is older than the American ones, and that the art of make-up was less advanced when the German film was made, this wonderful woman's face will hardly be recognizable. In the German film it is chalky and masklike, the skin looks muddy and gray, the eyes are expressionless, the hair seems dusty. In any of the American films her skin has a subdued satiny luster, her clear cool eyes are extraordinarily piercing, and her soft silky hair seems to glow with a mysterious inner radiance. By the help of clever lighting, irregular features can be made to look harmonious, a face can be made to look haggard or full, old or young. It is exactly the same with interiors and landscapes. Depending on the lighting, a room may look warm and comfortable, or cold and bare, large or small, clean or dirty; it may be striking at the first glance, or quite mediocre and insignificant. The effect of a bright beam of sunshine falling across a dark space could hardly be obtained with the same success in color. The strange fascination of a thundery landscape, the pallid light creeping in under a dark cover; the silhouette of a mountain range against the evening sky; the squalid grayness of an industrial area; waving cornfields; motes dancing in the sunshine between the shadows of tree trunks—all these are black-and-white effects by means of which desired moods may quite naturally be suggested in a narrative film. It is only necessary to remember the famous first act in Fritz Lang's *The Nibelungen Saga,* where Siegfried is riding through the magic forest.

The special delight in getting the sense of the texture of ordinary materials—such as dull iron, shining tin, smooth fur, the woolly hide of an animal, soft skin—in film or photograph is also heightened by the lack of hues. To be sure, texture is more faithfully reproducible in colors—as witness the famous paintings of silks by men like Terborch. If the art of giving the illusion of the reality of stuffs rouses great admiration even in painting, the effect is more uncannily exciting when it is obtained without the aid of color—simply in black and white. Occasionally a photographer succeeds in the supremely difficult art of registering surface qualities with an almost magical faithfulness, and thereby giving a particularly genuine picture of his subjects. On the other hand, one often notices how oddly a table set for a meal comes out in a film— what curious black things the people are eating, little blobs, and slimy-smooth shining balls and all kinds of flat things—they cut them up and put them cheerfully into their mouths, but one cannot see what they are.

Light, just as other properties of film, has been called to serve definite decorative and evocative purposes only as film developed into an art. In the early days any conspicuous light effect was avoided, just as perspective size-alterations and overlapping were shunned. If the effects of the lighting sprang to the eye too obviously in the picture, it was considered a professional error. The American director Cecil B. de Mille tells an instructive story to this effect:

"I had been accustomed to stage work, and I wanted to use a particular light effect, which I had used in the theater, for a film I was then shooting. In the scene in question, a spy came creeping through a curtain, and in order to make the effect more mysterious, I decided to light only half the spy's face and to leave the rest in darkness. I looked at the result on the screen and found it extraordinarily effective. I was so pleased with this trick of lighting that I used it throughout the film, that is, I used spotlights from one side or the other— a method which is now freely practiced. After I had sent the film to the distributor's office I got a telegram from the manager that surprised me considerably. It ran:—'Have you gone mad? Do you suppose we can sell a film for its full price if you only show half a man?'"

The film was rejected until de Mille hit on the idea of bluffing his customers by referring to the recondite authority of a great European artist. He wired back: "If you fellows are such fools that you don't know Rembrandt chiaroscuro when you see it, don't blame me." That did it. The distributor launched the film with the slogan: "The first film lighted in the Rembrandt style," asked double the usual price, and got it.

This story shows to what extent our way of seeing has changed in the last few years. Nowadays even the general public is accustomed to light effects such as those with which de Mille experimented then. But in those days film meant the reproduction of natural objects, and any formative intrusion was regarded as detracting from truth to nature, that is, from the fundamental object of film. A man who is only half visible is only half a man, and in real life men are never bisected—so Mr. de Mille's picture was no good. A simple equation. The lights must be so placed that all the details of every object would be clearly recognizable; no "disturbing" shadows were wanted but a clear survey. It was only later that the use of light in the service of art was learned.

ARTISTIC USE OF THE DELIMITATION OF THE PICTURE AND OF THE DISTANCE FROM THE OBJECT

Since our eyes can move freely in every direction, our field of vision is practically unlimited. A film image, on the other hand, is definitely bounded by its margins. Only what appears within these margins is visible, and therefore the film artist is forced—has the opportunity—to make a selection from the infinity of real life. In other words, he can choose his "motif." The delimitation of the image is as much a formative tool as perspective, for it allows of some particular detail being brought out and given special significance; and, conversely, of unimportant things being omitted, surprises being suddenly introduced into the shot, reflections of things that are happening "off" being brought in.

Moreover, a frame is an absolute essential if the decorative qualities of a picture are to be displayed; one can only consider the filling of the canvas, the allotment of space, and so forth, if there are definite limits to act as framework for the pictorial design. The frame of the image consists of two vertical and two horizontal lines. Every vertical and horizontal line occurring in the shot, therefore, will be supported by these axes. Slanting lines appear as slanting because the margins of the picture are straight, that is, vertical and horizontal; for every deviation requires some visible standard of comparison to show from what it deviates.

In a good film image, all lines and other directions stand in well-balanced relation to one another and to the margins. They support one another as parallels or are in contrast; they form a quiet or a restless pattern, a complicated or a simple one; and similarly with the distribution of dark and light masses. If the screen were infinitely large, there could be no question of a good organization of the surface, for, in order to achieve it, there must be a limited space to organize. There is no balance in the infinite, except perhaps in wallpaper designs where there is a serial uniformity, which, of course, is hardly applicable to the film.

The question of the size and proportion of the image is quite topical at present. Abel Gance in his Napoleon film took certain scenes for a triptych screen. At the performance three projectors operated simultaneously, so that a sort of panoramic strip resulted, which could be surveyed at a single glance only from a considerable distance. In America, too, various experiments have been made with enlarged screens. Nevertheless, the greater the surface of projection, the more difficult it is to organize the picture meaningfully. The temptation to increase the size of the screen goes with the desire for colored, stereoscopic, and sound film. It is the wish of people who do not know that artistic effect is bound up with the limitations of the medium and who want quantity rather than quality. They want to keep on getting nearer to nature and do not realize that they thereby make it increasingly difficult for film to be art.

The experiments with various-sized screens have once again raised the question as to how far the internationally standardized rectangular shape is artistically satisfactory. Statistical inquiries have been made to discover what shapes were preferred by the great masters. The Russian director Eisenstein during his stay in Hollywood gave a lecture advocating the square screen, within which horizontal and vertical rectangles of any proportion could be formed by using different-shaped masks. "Neither the vertical nor the horizontal shape alone is ideal," he said. "How may the vertical and horizontal tendencies of the film image be satisfied simultaneously? The battlefield for such a conflict is easily found—it is the square. The square is the only shape which is capable of producing all possible rectangles, if portions at the sides, or top and bottom are masked. It may also be used as a whole, in order to impress upon the spectator the cosmic finality of its squareness—particularly in a dynamic sequence of different dimensions, from a tiny square in the middle up to the all-embracing square that includes the whole screen."

In the beginnings of photography, and thus also of film art, only all-inclusive images were taken, that is, pictures that contained the whole of the event or object to be represented. Close-ups—a pair of hands, or half a face—could have been taken then as now, but they were not. Things that are technically possible are utilized only after the idea has penetrated that by their means useful and valuable results can be achieved, and not merely forbidden or unsound ones. If one wanted to take a shot of a man, his complete figure, or at least the whole upper part of his body, had to be in the picture. The margins of the screen were considered only in a negative sense—they must not cut parts of anything off. Interest was concentrated entirely on what was to be photographed, and not at all on the manner in which this was to be done. That sections and isolated details could be used creatively was a revolution, the same revolution that had to take place for all the other features of the film medium before it could become art. Just as Cecil B. de Mille's customers objected to having pictures in which faces were only partially illuminated, so it seemed absurd intentionally to cut up a natural object by the margins of the picture. Nowadays, after only a few years have passed, it has become fashionable even for quite mediocre directors to let the range finder go wild from time to time.

In the film *The Cameraman*, Buster Keaton is in love with a girl who works at a press-photograph agency. The following scene takes place: It is early morning. The office is being opened up, the employees arrive.

The reception room with the counter at which customers are received is shown. This is where the girl works. She enters, takes her coat off, and settles down. Suddenly the camera is shifted a little, and now a hitherto invisible corner of the waiting room comes into the picture, and there sits Buster Keaton, staring stupidly in front of him. He has been sitting there all night waiting to see the girl. This shows that even a long shot may actually be, in a sense, nothing but a detail shot. "Long shot" is of course a relative and inexact term, which cannot be defined, unless by saying: "A long shot includes the whole of everything that is relevant to the particular total situation." In practice it would be called a long shot if (as in this case) a whole office were shown. But that crucial corner occupied by Buster Keaton does not come into the picture and the whole effect of the shot depends on this. The same event might have been shown in this way: the girl comes up the stairs, opens the door into the office and sees Buster Keaton sitting in the corner. But the whole absurd and extravagant effect arises from the fact that the spectator believes to be seeing all there is to see—an ordinary office with ordinary people working in it—and suddenly, as if he had fallen from the skies, the ridiculous, infatuated boy is discovered, as though waiting from time immemorial in the midst of this businesslike office, in which nothing out of the ordinary is expected. The psychological shock which is given to the spectator might be described theoretically as follows: a complete whole is shown, and the spectator has been lulled to a false security; suddenly the total structure of this whole is altered by an insignificant twist which seems incongruous with what has gone before. Something of the same effect is achieved when Charlie Chaplin is seen in *Smart People* marvelously turned out in a top hat and tails; but only the upper part of his body is shown, and suddenly it is discovered that he has no trousers on and is standing there in his underpants. Here again the part that is shown (the upper part of the body) suggests a complete picture (smartly dressed man) and the disclosure shows in quite a different light what has already been seen, and turns it into a caricature.

Now for an example of an entirely different kind. Sternberg's *The Docks of New York* has a scene in which a suicide jumps off a boat. Nothing is shown in the shot except the quivering surface of the water in which is seen the reflection of the boat with the woman standing up and then jumping overboard. The woman is shown indirectly by her reflection in the water. The next moment, however, the woman herself is seen falling into the water, at the very spot where her reflection has been. This unexpected sequence of the direct upon the indirect view is most impressive. The effect is achieved by a careful choice of what is to be photographed. The camera is so placed that the most important part of the shot, namely, the boat with the woman on board, does not come in at all—a position which is quite absurd from the standpoint of ordinary representation of an object. The important part of the event, the only reason for which the shot has been taken, only throws its reflection into the picture. But the spectator, who perhaps might have watched a direct shot of the event with merely passing interest, is caught and thrilled by the unusualness of the presentation.

Similar artistic "tricks" are used frequently. They have almost become conventions—such as the shadow of the creeping villain appearing dark against a light wall. Indeed a shadow often acts as the announcer: it appears before the person throwing it comes on the scene, and by this means directs the audience's interest and attention to whatever is approaching.

The true virtue of the delimited image appears from the "close-up." The smaller the detail to be photographed, the larger it comes out in the picture. The close-up not only helps the artist give an enlargement of something which would not be obvious as a mere detail of a long shot—for example, that someone's eyes are filled with tears or that a mouse is sitting in a corner of a room—but it also takes some characteristic feature out of the whole. Very often the film artist will introduce his audience to a new situation by means of some such detail. The pendulum of a clock may be shown, then the whole clock, then the camera travels farther back, and people appear sitting in a room and looking anxiously at the clock. The clock is the vital point of the scene and is therefore shown first. In Pabst's *The Diary of a Lost Girl* the reformatory is introduced in the following manner: The hard, ill-natured face of the teacher with hair strained back from her forehead is shown first; then that she is rhythmically beating a gong; then the camera is moved back, and it is seen that she is standing at the head of a table at which the girls are having dinner, and are putting the spoons to their mouths in time to the strokes on the gong. Here again the central point, which is at the same time a detail illustrative of the situation, is picked out so as to direct the spectators' attention along the right lines, and also to provide a certain element of surprise; for a gradual revelation starting from the detail is much more exciting, seizes the spectators' interest much more than if the whole scene were given at once.

A sequence of scenes leading like this from the detail to the total picture can be given in various ways. Either the whole and the detail can be taken separately and joined together in the finished strip, in which case the shots go from one to the next with a jerk; or else the camera is moved backward, the shot being continuously turned, so that what appears on the screen becomes at the same time smaller and more comprehensive—that is, the detail which was at first large becomes gradually small and slips into its place in the whole scene. Or, thirdly, the camera may be left in position, while the operator works with mobile masks, so that at first the greater part of the picture remains dark and some detail of the scene—say a head—is seen in a small (round) setting, as if through a hole in a curtain. Starting from this hole, then, the whole shot "fades in."

There are still other ways of using close-ups, and these are much less easy to fit into any definite scheme. In *The Docks of New York* there is a love scene between a sailor and a prostitute. They are sitting drinking, and there is not much sign of love. Then a close-up is cut in, an uncannily lewd detail: she lustfully strokes his naked arm with indecent tattoo marks all over it, as he ripples the muscles on it for her amusement. The same scene taken as a long shot would not be nearly as effective. Instead of the whole man, only his arm appears, a sturdy, naked, lewdly decorated thing—a clever application of the principle of *pars pro toto:* this woman sees nothing of the man but power, nudity, muscle.

Similar examples can be found in any film: the feet of a man going upstairs, so as to indicate visually the sound of the steps; the legs of a couple of lovers. Feyder's *Les Nouveaux Messieurs* has a scene depicting the ceremonial opening of a number of new buildings in a workmen's colony. The Minister is in a hurry and makes his inspection more and more rapidly, until the whole procession is positively running. Then comes a close-up: a fat man in the procession, no one in particular, mopping his brow. This man has been picked out as the type of all his fellow sufferers. In Pudovkin's *Mother* the scenes taking place in the law courts are ushered in by rapidly successive close-ups of the cold gray ashlars of the building, and in one case a huge shot of the boot of one of the soldiers on guard, a dark uncanny apparition, which is an excellent introduction to the mood of the following scenes. The Russians, indeed, have created an entirely new technique of close-ups.

The possibility of varying the range of the image and the distance from the object thus provides the film artist with the means of splitting up the whole of any scene easily without interfering with reality. Parts may represent the whole, suspense may be created by leaving what is important or remarkable out of the picture. Certain portions may be emphasized so as to induce the spectator to seek symbolic meaning in their appearance. Particular attention may be focused on essential details.

The close-up, however, has one serious drawback. It easily leaves the spectator in the dark as to the surroundings of the object or part of the object. This is especially true in a film where there are too many close-ups, where hardly any long shots are given, as for instance in Dreyer's *The Passion of Joan of Arc,* or in a number of Russian films. The close-up shows a human head, but one cannot tell where the man is to whom the head belongs, whether he is indoors or outdoors, and how he is placed in regard to other people—whether close or distant, turning toward them or away from them, in the same room with them or somewhere else. A superabundance of close-ups very easily leads to the spectators having a tiresome sense of uncertainty and dislocation. Thus a film artist will generally find himself obliged not to use close-ups alone but only in conjunction with long shots that will give the necessary information as to the situation in general.

On the other hand, however, the film artist has a valuable means of expression, which is denied to the stage, in the power of choosing his distance from his subject. In a theater the spectator always remains at the same distance from the scene of action, and hence events and objects can only be shown within certain limits of size. The subtleties of facial expression, for instance, are lost for the majority of the spectators, who are not seated close to the stage. Indeed unless gifted with very sharp eyes or by making use of the unsatisfactory, because falsifying, assistance of opera glasses, the audience even in the first balcony will be able to catch only a fraction of what is shown on the stage.

It is, however, not only technical matters of visual acuity that are under discussion. The constant distance of the spectator from the stage makes for an unchangeable evaluation of properties and actions on the stage "according to size," which is most important aesthetically. From a visual standpoint the movements of the actors, their costumes, the sets, are only effective up to a fairly low degree of differentiation. Film can enlarge this range of validity and, which is more important, it can shift it. The spectator may have been looking at a whole room but the next minute the camera can provide quite a different scene on the same spot, in which quite different things form the center of interest, quite different objects come out large and important, and possibly everything that was important in the long shot a moment ago has been omitted. Of a room containing two people only a tiny half-yard-square patch of the table remains and lying on it a flower that had before been unnoticed or, in any case, had taken up only a minute portion of the picture. Toward this flower, now the center of the action, grope the fingers of a hand, equally large, equally important, which was small and inconspicuous and played no part previously.

The sphere of operation of the film compared with that of the theater is thereby enormously enlarged. It must be added that, even if it were technically possible, emphasis upon the nonhuman element in the theater would be hardly appropriate. The theater depends on the spoken word; ordinary dramatic scenes, whose meaning lies in the dialogue, could never combine to give a homogeneous effect with scenes in which inarticulate things like animals or flowers carried on the action simply by their appearance or by movements accompanied or unaccompanied by sounds. Anything of this kind is only very exceptionally possible on the stage; and even in the kind of sound film that is based essentially on dialogue the introduction of such scenes at important points would produce a disturbing and incoherent effect.

Perhaps the point has never been made explicitly—and it seems significant that it occurs to very few theatergoers—how unnatural, how stylized, all stage art is because the actors never stop talking. Every action is overlaid and clothed with words. Even in the first outline, every scene is so planned that the plot shall be unfolded by unceasing conversation. Indeed every preponderance of mere action over the spoken word is regarded as a defect. The spoken word, the most important distinguishing trait of the drama, has developed into a medium of radical purity during the evolution of the art through thousands of years. That this method of presenting an event is not a matter of course will be clearly realized only after seeing from a good silent film how the action proceeds quite easily without any use of words at all.

Film can make inanimate objects attract attention to themselves. Let us suppose again that in a particular scene on the stage a flower is lying on a table. This flower could never, except with the help of the actors, attract the attention of the audience. The stage director or the playwright cannot rely on the possibility that the audience might in the course of the play notice the insignificant detail because the audience's attention must always be directed to the precise point of the action.

The film artist has the best possible control of his audience's attention; for by placing the camera just where he wishes he brings onto the screen whatever is of greatest importance at the time, and is able to give proper significance to objects without there being any need for the flower to call out "Now look at me." The interest of the spectator is necessarily directed to it because at the time he is shown nothing else. Similarly other small events—a fly crawling, or the smoke of a cigarette—which would not be nearly emphatic enough on the stage to draw attention to themselves are given the requisite stress.

In a film, these little events, these roles played by accessories, are exactly of the same type as the "macroscopic" ones, those represented by the human actors. And hence arises a most satisfactory homogeneity.

The possibility of rapidly changing the distance from the object leads naturally to a relativization of the standards of size. Insofar as the spectator cannot use his past experience to judge what he sees—insofar as he does not know, for instance, that a fly is objectively small and a mountain large—he has nothing to go on in judging the objective size of what is shown. He has no means of knowing how far the camera stood from the object. A newsreel of an architectural exhibition showed several shots of houses that had been erected on the grounds, and immediately afterward, shots of a little plaster model of the city of Rome. To the spectator both sets of buildings appeared of equal size, although in one they were of ordinary height and taken at the necessary distance, and in the other the models were only a few inches high and photographed close to. Experience was here of no use to the spectator in judging the relative sizes.

This relativization results, on the one hand, in the possibility of making things of quite different sizes appear the same size, and thus of being brought into connection one with another. In a film on German university life the rounded belly of a corps student, who is snoring on a sofa, dissolves into a landscape shot —a similarly formed, gently rounded hill near Heidelberg. These two things which actually are of totally different sizes are simply and easily made to coalesce by the stomach being photographed from close to and the hill from far away; and thereby the opportunity is given of making an amusing comparison between them.

On the other hand, particular effects may be induced by the spectators being deceived as to the real size of what is shown. A critic once referred to a scene in the film version of Ibsen's *A Doll's House* as a standard example of the idiom of film art. A room is shown, and suddenly a huge hand is put into it, and thereby it is made clear that the room is actually quite small and only part of a doll's house. At first glance the room is assumed to be of normal size, for in the picture itself there is nothing to indicate that anything exceptional—a toy—is involved. The sudden change brought about by perfectly natural means— the normal-sized human hand—brings home the symbolism of the happening to the spectator in the best way. What is only a conceptual identification of the human house and the toy house actually takes place here. Thus once again a "drawback" in film—the im-

possibility of giving any absolute standard of size—
is turned to advantage, and used for artistic effect.

ARTISTIC USE OF THE ABSENCE OF THE
SPACE-TIME CONTINUUM

Unlike real life, film permits of jumps in time and
space. Montage means joining together shots of situations that occur at different times and in different
places. Theorists, and especially the Russians, have
hitherto investigated montage more thoroughly than
any other branch of film art.

It was the Russians who first realized the artistic
potentialities of montage; and it was they who first
made an attempt to define its principles systematically. At the same time they have often carried
their enthusiasm for it too far. They are inclined
to consider montage as the only important artistic
film feature—as witness their frequently excessive
use of it. Indeed the impression is sometimes left
that they consider a single uncut strip of film simply
a piece of reality—as though an edited film were,
so to speak, cut nature. Pudovkin begins his book
Film Technique with the statement that montage
is the foundation of film art. We have tried to show
above how even a single shot is in no sense a simple
reproduction of nature; how even in the single shot
most important differences exist between nature and
the film image; and how seriously artistic formative
processes must be considered.

It can be easily seen, however, why montage might
be thought of as the royal road to film art. The single
image, after all, arises from a recording process, which

is controlled by man but which, regarded superficially, does no more than reproduce nature. But when it comes to montage man takes a hand in the process— time is broken up, things that are disconnected in time and space are joined together. This looks much more like a tangibly creative and formative process.

Pudovkin describes the beginnings of film art as follows: "There was no room for art in the work of the photographer. He photographed the art of the performers. There was of course no question of any special art of film acting, of any particular attributes of film or of methods of approach for the director. What actually was the work of the director in those days? He had the script, which was exactly like a play written for the theater—except that there were no words, and an attempt was made to fill their place with gesture and often lengthy subtitles. The director treated the scene as if it were one on the stage; he arranged entrances and exits, the transitions, and other movements of the actors. He had the whole of such a scene played, while the camera man recorded it in its entirety—the camera simply served to fixate scenes that were complete and finished in themselves." Montage only arrived with the development of film as an art.

Montage of an event coherent in time and space must be distinguished from the crosscutting of events that are dissociated from each other. It was with the latter that montage began historically, because it is the less revolutionary process; the different shots were joined to each other, just as different scenes were acted in sequence on the stage. On the stage it had been the custom for hundreds of years to show sequences of scenes that had no connection in time or place. Then came something of which only the rudiments existed on the stage: the scenes were cut up and the various parts mixed in with one another— that is, the action was suddenly interrupted, quite a different scene was played, then this was interrupted and the first continued, then the second again, and so on. The beginnings of this procedure can be found in traditional drama, where, for example, in Shakespearian battle scenes the action often alternated between one camp and the other. In a film the procedure was much easier to use because, instead of having actually to reset the scene on the stage, one scene could follow the next in a smooth rapid sequence.

It was a much bolder stroke to intervene in one unitary scene, to split up an event, to change the position of the camera in midstream, to bring it nearer, move it farther away, to alter the selection of the subject matter shown. This has up to the present been the most vigorous and stimulating move toward the emancipation of the camera.

In montage the film artist has a first-class formative instrument, which helps him to emphasize and give greater significance to the actual events that he portrays. From the time continuum of a scene he takes only the parts that interest him, and of the spatial totality of objects and events he picks out only what is relevant. Some details he stresses, others he omits altogether. Examples of this have already been given above.

Sometimes, too, shots are associated by montage whose connection is not realistic but conceptual or poetic. "I wished to depict joy filmically. Merely to photograph a face registering joy would have been totally ineffective. So I showed the play of the hands and a close-up of the lower half of the face, of the smiling mouth. I cut-in various other material to this; for instance, a shot of a rushing brook in springtime, with dancing sunbeams reflected in the water; of birds splashing in the village pond; and, finally, of a laughing child. I felt I had thus expressed 'The joy of the prisoner.'" The artistic fitness of such a sequence is disputable. The scene comes from Pudovkin's *Mother*. His contempt for the uncut picture, the raw material, is very characteristic—although this attitude is found only in Russian theory and not at all in practice: the Russians understand so well how to choose their material. It is, moreover, very questionable whether the symbolic connection of smile, brook, sunbeams, "happy prisoner," and "joyous child" can add up to visual unity. It has been done thousands of times in poetry; but disconnected themes can easily be joined in language because the mental images attached to words are much vaguer, more abstract and will therefore more readily cohere. Putting actual pictures in juxtaposition, especially in an otherwise realistic film, often appears forced. The unity of the scene, the story of the prisoner who is rejoicing, is suddenly interrupted by something totally different. Comparisons and associations like the brook and the sunbeams are not lightly touched upon in the abstract but are introduced as concrete pieces of nature—and hence are distracting.

Apart from whether this single instance has been successful or not, the fact remains that the possibility of this kind of montage exists; and one of its dis-

tinguishing features is that the shots which follow
one another have no space-time connection but only
one of substance. It would be quite pointless to inquire whether the brook flows after the face has
smiled, or how far from the laughing child are the
birds splashing in the water. It is the artist's job to
present the material in such a way that the spectators
approach it with the correct attitude: they must not
be looking for time-space connections. On the other
hand, one often finds that unity of place is intended,
but that owing to clumsy editing the effect of unity
is lost. A man appears and then a second one; and
there is nothing to show that these people are supposed to be in the same place. It looks as though
the scene had changed to somewhere else and it is
impossible to understand what connection there is between the two figures. Since montage separates things
that are spatially continuous and joins together things
that have no inherent space-time continuity, the danger arises that the process may not be successful
and that the whole may disintegrate into pieces, which
the spectator cannot combine according to the artist's
plan.

Pudovkin has laid down five methods of montage;
but the system does not appear altogether satisfactory
logically because the classification refers partly to the
manner of cutting and partly to the subject matter,
and these two factors are not kept separate.

1) *Contrast*

"The miserable state of a starving man is to be
shown, for instance. The narrative will make an even
greater impression if his condition is contrasted with

one of lavish wealth." (Again the strange distrust of uncut material.) This gives no hint of the technique of cutting—whether the two scenes are to follow entire one upon the other or are to be interlaced piecemeal.

2) *Parallelism*

"The method is similar to that of contrast, but it goes much further." The two different kinds of events are shown alternately by single shots. Obviously, the logical coördination is false. The method of contrast referred to subject matter—the method of parallelism deals with the technique of cutting.

3) *Similarity*

"In the finale of *Ştrike* by Eisenstein workmen are being shot down and the scene is cut to the slaughter of an ox in a stockyard." This category once more refers to the content. In principle it does not matter whether interlacing montage or a sequence of whole scenes is used. The first procedure would probably as a rule be more obviously effective.

4) *Synchronism*

Two parallel events, related to each other because they occur at the same time. For instance, someone hurries home to rescue his friend, who is led to the scaffold. The interest lies in wondering whether the spatial coincidence will take place soon enough. A third principle is introduced here, to which no reference has been made before. Under none of the preceding headings was anything said about the time connection between the scenes that were cut-in with one another.

5) *Recurrent theme* (*Leitmotiv*)

"If the script writer wishes to stress the basic theme underlying his scenario, the method of reiteration will be of great assistance to him." The particular scene recurs several times in the same form as a sort of "refrain"—once again referring almost entirely to the content.

The above is really a bad scheme of classification. Timoshenko, in turn, lays down fifteen principles of montage as follows:

1) Change of place
2) Change of position of the camera
3) Change of range of image
4) Stressing of details
5) Analytical montage
6) Return to past time
7) Anticipation of the future
8) Parallel events
9) Contrast
10) Association
11) Concentration
12) Enlargement
13) Monodramatic montage
14) Refrain
15) Montage

Since it also it not very satisfactory, this classification will not be discussed further here. It is nothing but an incomplete and unsystematic enumeration of factors, some of which should not be coördinated but subordinated logically.

In the following, another scheme is attempted, into which the main points of Pudovkin's and Timoshenko's classifications are worked.

PRINCIPLES OF MONTAGE

I. *Principles of Cutting*
   A. Length of the cutting unit
      1) Long strips. (The shots that are joined together are all relatively long. Quiet rhythm.)
      2) Short strips. (. . . are all relatively short. Usually employed in cases where the shots themselves are full of rapid action. Climactic scenes. Effect of tumult. Quick rhythm.)
      3) Combination of short and long—into long strips suddenly one or more quite short pieces. Or vice versa. Corresponding rhythm.
      4) Irregular—series of strips of variable length, neither definitely short nor long. The length dependent on the contents. No rhythmic effect.
   B. Montage of whole scenes
      1) Sequential. (An action played straight through to the end. The next joined to it, and so on.)
      2) Interlaced. (The scenes are cut up small and these parts are fitted in with one another. Alternate continuation of one and the other scene. Crosscutting.)
      3) Insertion (of scenes or single frames in a continuous action).

C. Montage within an individual scene

1) Combination of long shots and close-ups. (By long shot, which is a relative term, is to be understood one which puts the subject of the close-up in a wider context.)

    a) First a long shot, then one or more details of it as close-ups. (Timoshenko's "concentration.")

    b) Proceeding from one detail (or several) to a long shot including this detail. (Timoshenko's "enlargement.") For instance, in the example from Pabst's *The Diary of a Lost Girl*, first the head of the teacher, then the whole dining room.

    c) Long shots and close-ups in irregular succession.

2) Succession of detail shots (of which none includes the subject of the others). (Timoshenko's "analytical montage.") A whole event or a passing situation composed of nothing but small pieces.

As, in IB, in the combining of whole scenes, so here within the individual scenes, montage may be used for succession, crosscutting, or insertion.

II. *Time Relations*

A. Synchronism

1) of several entire scenes (Timoshenko's "parallel events"; Pudovkin's "synchronism") joined in sequence or crosscut. In sequences usually connected by continuity titles: "While this occurred in X, in Y . . ."

2) of details of a setting of action at the same mo-

ment of time. (Successive showing of events taking place at the same time in the same place. The man is here, the woman there, etc.) (Timoshenko's "analytical montage.") Unusable.

B. Before, after

1) Whole scenes, succeeding each other in time. But also inserted scenes of what has happened ("memory") or of things that will happen in the future ("prophetic vision"). (Timoshenko's "return to past time" and "anticipation of the future.")

2) Succession within a scene. Succession of details which succeed one another in time within the whole action. For example: first shot—he seizes the revolver; second shot—she runs away.

C. Neutral

1) Complete actions that are not connected in time but only as regards content. Eisenstein: The shooting of workmen by soldiers cut-in with an ox being slaughtered in a stockyard. Before? After?

2) Single shots that have no time connection. Rare in narrative films; but, e.g., in Vertov's documentaries.

3) Inclusion of single shots in a complete scene. For example, Pudovkin's symbolic montage: "joy of the prisoner." Shots inserted without time connection with the event.

III. *Space Relations*

A. The same place (though different time)

1) In whole scenes. Someone returns to the same

place twenty years later. The two scenes succeeding each other or crosscut.

2) Within a single scene. "Compressed time." A
leap forward in time so that one sees in unbroken succession what is happening in the
same place but actually after a lapse of time.
Unusable.

B. The place changed
1) Whole scenes. Succession or interlacing of
scenes which occur at different places.
2) Within one scene. Different partial views of
the place of action.
3) Neutral.
The same as IIC (1–3)

IV. *Relations of Subject Matter*
A. Similarity
1) of shape
   a) of an object. (A round hillock follows on
   the rounded belly of a student.)
   b) of a movement. (A playground swing in
   motion follows on the swinging pendulum
   of a clock.)
2) of meaning
   a) Single object. (Pudovkin's montage: Laughing prisoner, brook, birds bathing, happy
   child.)
   b) Whole scene. (Eisenstein: The workmen
   are shot down, the ox is slaughtered.)
B. Contrast
1) of shape
   a) of an object. (First a very fat man, then a
   thin one.)

> > *b*) of movement. (A slow movement following
> > on a very rapid one.)
> 2) of meaning
> > *a*) Single object. (A starving unemployed man;
> > a shop window full of delicious food.)
> > *b*) Whole scene. (In the house of a rich man;
> > in the house of a poor one.)
> C. Combination of similarity and contrast
> > 1) Similarity of shape and contrast of meaning.
> > (Timoshenko: The feet of a prisoner fettered
> > in a dungeon, and the legs of dancers in a
> > theater. Or: the rich man in an armchair, the
> > rebel in the electric chair.)
> > 2) Similarity of meaning and contrast of form.
> > (Something of this sort in *Buster Keaton as
> > Sherlock Holmes Junior*. He sees a huge pic-
> > ture on the screen of a couple kissing each
> > other, and kisses his girl in the operator's box.)

This scheme is not intended to be exhaustive, and
certainly is not so. It is only meant to be a skeleton,
to give a general survey.

The principles under IV may be supplemented by
the following remarks: if strips of film are joined one
to another, it is often observed, especially with really
good montage, that they do not simply stand "ad-
ditively" beside one another but take on quite different shades of meaning through this juxtaposition. Thus
in Eisenstein's scene to which we have already referred
the shooting down of the workmen receives a very
definite shade of meaning from being combined with
the slaughterhouse scene.

Similarly the purely formal aspect of a picture is

often greatly influenced by montage. If the figure of a very tall man is shown directly after a very short one, this tall man is regarded by the spectator quite otherwise than if he had been shown alone: his height is particularly emphasized by the contrast. This influence may sometimes go so far as to make shots that are placed one after the other appear to be continuous—thus, for instance, the feeling of seeing two separate shots, first of a short man and then a tall one, might be completely lost, and instead the small man be seen to grow tall with a jerk, that is, to shoot upward. If one sees a fat round face and directly afterward a long narrow one, the impression is easily given that the first face has been pulled out and has suddenly grown long and thin. Similar results have been attained in experimental psychology. In his investigation of "illusory movement" Max Wertheimer has described experiments in which he let two illuminated slots, at a small distance from each other, bob up in rapid succession before the eyes of a person in a darkened room. If the distance and the exposure time were correctly chosen, the person had the overwhelming impression that there were not two separate slots lighting up one after the other and beside each other, but that *one* slot appeared on the left, ran over to the right and was there extinguished.

This stroboscopic fusion of objectively separate stimuli into one unified impression also occurs in film by montage. In fact, fundamentally, the whole existence of the motion picture is dependent on this principle. For actually, objectively, there is nothing but a succession of single motionless images, phases of motion, on the celluloid strip. It is only because the images succeed one another so rapidly and because they fit one another so exactly that the impression of continuous movement is given. Fundamentally, therefore, film is the montage of single frames—imperceptible montage. Carrying over this principle to the macroscopic, so to speak, results in the above-mentioned effects. If in the first shot a face is shown in profile and in the second full face, the spectator may get the impression that a face has turned toward him.

Use has already been made of this phenomenon here and there for artistic purposes. There is a well-known scene in Eisenstein's *The Battleship Potemkin,* which shows a stone lion rearing up and roaring. The scene is made from shots of three different statues of lions. First statue—a lion crouching. Second statue—a lion rising. Third statue—a lion standing with his jaws open to roar. The way the stone comes to life by the help of editing is most remarkable.

A similar effect is attempted in Karl Junghans' *Life's Like That.* First shot—the statue of a saint with crossed arms. Second shot—a similar statue with arms stretched up to heaven. The effect—with a symbolic meaning—is that the saint is alive and has given a sign.

This principle leads to tricks of montage, where it is no longer a case of fitting together shots that are unrelated in time and space, but where unity of action is so strong that one does not notice that montage has been employed, and, therefore, perceives the resulting phenomena as actual happenings. If several frames are omitted from a scene showing a man going for a walk, the impression on the spectator is that the man has suddenly with lightning rapidity been picked out of his stride and pushed onward; one does not notice that this effect is achieved merely by joining together disconnected pictures.

It is perhaps just as well not to designate this process as montage, so as to emphasize that a totally different artistic device is in question than in the methods previously discussed. Montage, in the real sense of the word, requires that the spectator should observe the discrepancy among the shots that are joined together; it is intended to group slices of reality in an integrated whole, whereas the process which was mentioned just now does not unite disconnected things but changes the nature of one continuous action.

Whereas montage proper does not interfere with the reality material photographed in the picture, the process now under discussion does interfere with it, makes it appear different. Actual events are changed, new realities created. People can be made to appear or disappear suddenly (Chaplin has employed this trick; the French surrealists such as René Clair also used it—a man stretches out a magic wand and the people round him vanish). A sort of accelerated motion can also be achieved; for instance, one scene in the film *Market in Berlin* by Wilfried Basse undertakes to show how the booths are built up in the empty square. He achieves his effect very cleverly by joining together shots taken at intervals of half an hour so that one sees the booths springing up by jerks. Within a few seconds the square is magically covered with booths more and more densely until the picture of the market is complete. This method of "imperceptible montage" can, nevertheless, also be used for scenes which do not give such a supernatural effect. It is conceivable that the sudden turning of a person's head, a movement of flight, or something of the same sort, might be more impressively shown by cutting a few frames out of the strip and thus achieving a jerk within the movement. That inanimate things may be made mobile to a certain degree was shown above in the example of the stone lions.

ARTISTIC USE OF THE ABSENCE OF NONVISUAL SENSE EXPERIENCES

One of the factors that determine the difference between looking at a motion picture and looking at reality is the absence of the sense of balance and other kinesthetic experiences. In everyday life we always know whether we are looking straight ahead or up or down; we know whether our body is at rest or in motion, and in what kind of motion. But, as was pointed out before, the spectator cannot tell from what angle a film shot has been taken. Hence, unless the subject matter tells him otherwise, he assumes that the camera was at rest and that it was shooting straight. If a moving object appears in the shot, the spectator's first assumption will be that the object is really in motion and not simply that the camera is running past a stationary object. And as far as the space coördinates are concerned, his first idea will always be that what appears at the top of the screen was also on top at the place that was photographed, and not that the camera might have been inclined at an angle.

Use is made of relativity of movement, for instance,

in those scenes from *Dr. Mabuse* in which, in order to demonstrate the power of the mysterious man, his face appears small against a dark background, glides forward swiftly, growing larger, until it becomes so huge that it occupies the whole screen. In taking the shot, however, the face was presumably not moved toward the camera, but the camera toward the face. In the Russian film, *The Shanghai Document*, shots of a horse race are seen. The horses and their jockeys are shown galloping over the track, with cuts every now and then to very effective shots of a fluttering flag bearing a racing horse and its rider. The waving of the flag gives the effect of the horse moving; and since the flag (in a close-up) entirely fills the screen, and thus the surroundings do not show that the flag and its horse are actually at rest, it looks as though the horse were galloping and the camera were racing beside it. A subtle (and moreover extremely effective) trick— the illusion of an illusion; for the illusion of standstill which comes of the camera pursuing an actually moving object at the same pace is imitated by a cleverly taken shot of an object that is actually at rest. And the beauty of the idea is that the artifice whereby the spectator is made to feel that the apparently motionless object may be only relatively so, may indeed be actually moving, has not been arbitrarily dragged in but has been achieved in the most natural way by the fluttering of the flag.

In Murnau's *The Four Devils* there is a circus scene: A white horse trots steadily round the arena, the camera follows, and so the horse always remains in the middle of the screen and seems almost stationary, because only its body and not its legs are seen; but the whole circle of the auditorium glides past panoramically in the background.

The apparent movement in the shot which is due to the motion of the camera has been very cleverly used by Pabst in *The Beggar's Opera,* in order to emphasize the fantastic and unreal quality of his film.

The absence of any feeling of the force of gravity also makes a worm's-eye view particularly compelling. If, for instance, a human being is photographed from below, it is of course obvious from the shot that the camera has been directed upward, but this recognition is not quite absorbed by perception—the spectator still feels very strongly that the picture plane is vertical and therefore the figure slanting. The figure appears to be inclined backward; the longitudinal axis of the figure does not appear vertical but oblique, sloping from the bottom front to the top back. Diagram 1 shows the actual circumstances of the case; the human figure (AB) is upright, the camera (CD) inclined at an angle (fig. 1). But as there is nothing to show the spectator that the camera was inclined, he supposes (fig. 2) that CD was upright and therefore sees AB as slanting. This effect helps to make a slanting view very much more striking than it would appear in real life.

The relativity of the spatial framework could be exploited, as shown in Diagram 2. A man (AB) standing upright, is taken by a camera (CD) directed in the normal horizontal manner (fig. 1); and this photograph is now dissolved into that of a recumbent man who is taken from above (fig. 2). On the screen, the directions in both shots would look alike (fig. 3).

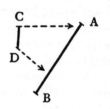

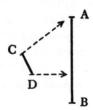

Figure 1   Figure 2

DIAGRAM 1

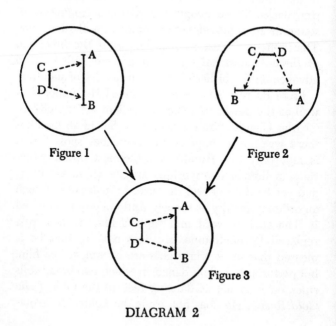

Figure 1   Figure 2

Figure 3

DIAGRAM 2

A man would be seen, upright and with his head at the top of the screen, though it might appear from the subject matter that the second man was really recumbent. If there were some good reason for it in the plot this might be most effective—for example, fading a soldier on sentry duty into a dead man lying on the ground.

Thereby, again, a "defect" of photographic technique—the inability to realize the correct space coördinates purely from the appearance of a picture—would have been used to achieve an artistic effect.

People who did not understand anything of the art of film used to cite silence as one of its most serious drawbacks. These people regard the introduction of sound as an improvement or completion of silent film. This opinion is just as senseless as if the invention of three-dimensional oil painting were hailed as an advance on the hitherto known principles of painting.

From its very silence film received the impetus as well as the power to achieve excellent artistic effects. Charles Chaplin wrote somewhere that in all his films there was not a single scene where he "spoke," that is, moved his lips. Hundreds of the most various situations in human relationships are shown in his films, and yet he did not feel the need to make use of such an ordinary faculty as speech. And nobody has missed it. The spoken word in Chaplin's films is as a rule replaced by pantomine. He does not *say* that he is pleased that some pretty girls are coming to see him, but performs the silent dance, in which two bread rolls stuck on forks act as dancing feet on the table (*The Gold Rush*). He does not argue, he fights. He avows his love by smiling, swaying his shoulders, and moving his hat. When he is in the pulpit he does not preach in words, but acts the story of David and Goliath (*The Pilgrim*). When he is sorry for a poor girl, he stuffs money into her handbag. He shows renunciation by simply walking away (finale of *The Circus*). The incredible visual concreteness of every one of his scenes makes for a great part of Chaplin's art; and this should not be forgotten when it is said—as is often done and of course not without foundation—that his films are not really "filmic" (because his camera serves mainly as a recording machine).

Mention has already been made of the scene from Sternberg's *The Docks of New York* in which a revolver shot is illustrated by the rising of a flock of birds. Such an effect is not just a contrivance on the part of a director to deal with the evil of silence by using an indirect visual method of explaining to the audience that there has been a bang. On the contrary, a positive artistic effect results from the paraphrase. Such indirect representation of an event in a material that is strange to it, or giving not the action itself but only its consequences, is a favorite method in all art. To take an example at random: when Francesca da Rimini tells how she fell in love with the man with whom she was in the habit of reading, and only says "We read no more that day," Dante thereby indicates indirectly, simply by giving the consequences, that on this day they kissed each other. And this indirectness is shockingly impressive.

In the same way, the rising of the birds is particularly effective, and probably more so than if the actual sound of the pistol shot were heard. And then another factor comes in: the spectator does not simply *infer* that a shot has been fired, but he actually *sees* something of the quality of the noise—the suddenness, the abruptness of the rising birds, give visually the exact quality that the shot possesses acoustically. In Jacques Feyder's *Les Nouveaux Messieurs* a political meeting becomes very uproarious, and in order to calm the rising emotions Suzanne puts a coin into a mechanical piano. Immediately the hall is lit up by hundreds of electric bulbs, and now the music chimes in with the agitative speech. The music is not heard: it is a silent film. But Feyder shows the audience excitedly listening to the speaker; and suddenly the faces soften and relax; all the heads begin quite gently to sway in time to the music. The rhythm grows more pronounced until at last the spirit of the dance has seized them all; and they swing their bodies gaily from side to side as if to an unheard word of command. The speaker has to give way to the music. Much more clearly than if the music were actually heard, this shows the power that suddenly unites all these discontented people, puts them into the same merry mood; and indicates as well the character of the music itself, its sway and rhythm. What is particularly noteworthy in such a scene is not merely how easily and cleverly the director makes visible something that is not visual, but by so doing, actually strengthens its effect. If the music were really heard, the spectator might simply realize that music was sounding, but by this indirect method, the particular point, the important part of this music—its rhythm, its power to unite and "move" men—is conspicuously brought out.

Only these special attributes of the music are given, and appear as the music itself. Similarly the fact that a pistol shot is sudden, explosive, startling, becomes doubly impressive by transposition into the visible, because only these particular attributes and not the shot itself are given. Thus silent film derives definite artistic potentialities from its silence. What it wishes particularly to emphasize in an audible occurrence is transposed into something visual; and thus instead of giving the occurrence "itself," it gives only some of its telling characteristics, and thereby shapes and interprets it.

Owing to its insubstantiality silent film does not in any way give the effect of being dumb pantomime. Its silence is not noticed, unless the action happens to culminate in something acoustic for which nothing can be substituted, and which is therefore felt as missing—or unless one is accustomed to sound film. Because of sound film, in the future it will be possible only with great difficulty to show speech in a silent way. Yet this is a most effective artistic device. For if a man is heard speaking, his gestures and facial expression only appear as an accompaniment to underline the sense of what is said. But if one does not hear what is said, the meaning becomes indirectly clear and is artistically interpreted by muscles of the face, of the limbs, of the body. The emotional quality of the conversation is made obvious with a clarity and definiteness which are hardly possible in the medium of actual speech. Moreover, the divergence between reality and dumb show gives the actor and his director plenty of leeway for artistic invention. (The creative power of the artist can only come into play where reality and the medium of representation do not coincide.)

Dialogue in silent film is not simply the visible part of a real spoken dialogue. If a real dialogue is shown without the sound, the spectator will often fail to grasp what it is all about; he will find the facial expression and the gestures unintelligible. In silent film, the lips are no longer word-forming physical organs but a means of visual expression—the distortion of an excited mouth or the fast chatter of lips are not mere by-products of talking; they are communications in their own right. Silent laughter is often more effective than if the sound is actually heard. The gaping of the open mouth gives a vivid, highly artistic interpretation of the phenomenon "laughter." If, however, the sound is also heard, the opening of the mouth appears obvious and its value as a means of expression is almost entirely lost. This opportunity of the silent film was once used by the Russians in a most unusual and effective manner. A shot of a soldier who had gone mad in the course of a battle and was laughing hideously with his mouth wide open was joined with a shot of the body of a soldier who had died of poison gas, and whose mouth was fixed in death in a ghastly, rigid grin.

The absence of the spoken word concentrates the spectator's attention more closely on the visible aspect of behavior, and thus the whole event draws particular interest to itself. Hence it is that very ordinary shots are often so impressive in silent films—such as a documentary shot of an itinerant hawker crying his wares with grandiose gestures. If his words could be heard the effect of the gestures would not be half as great, and the whole episode might attract very little attention. If, however, the words are omitted, the spectator surrenders entirely to the expressive power of the gestures. Thus by merely robbing the real event of something—the sound—the appeal of such an episode is greatly heightened.

Except for such a highly gesticulatory figure as the hawker, a dialogue taken straight from real life seldom conveys much in silent film. One can extract from such a strip distinctive little parts such as are to be found in practically every dialogue, but even this process of selection only leads to accidental success. Hence, too, the difficulty of many stage players to adapt themselves to the technique of silent film; and also the fact that certain techniques which actors acquire in film work look embarrassing on the stage.

OTHER CAPACITIES OF FILM TECHNIQUE

1) *The Mobile Camera*

Hitherto we have discussed chiefly the fixed camera. But it is well known that the camera can be placed on a truck, or slide along a cable, or be tilted and rotated for "panning." The subject of the shot increases in size when the camera approaches it, and at the same time the range of the field is diminished. This makes possible an unbroken change from a long shot to a close-up, and vice versa, without any necessity for montage.

The moving camera is especially useful when the scene of action is not an immobile setting, in which the actors come and go, but the actors are, as it were, the constant setting while the surroundings vary. The camera may accompany the hero through all the rooms of a house, down the stairs, along the street; and the human figure may always remain the same, while the surroundings pass as a panorama, continually changing. The film artist is thereby able to do what is very hard for the theater director, namely, to show the world from the standpoint of an individual, to take man as the center of his cosmos—that is, to make a very subjective experience accessible to the eyes of all.

Indeed, experiences of an even more subjective nature may be represented in this manner. How "everything seems to turn round" someone, feelings of giddiness, vertigo, intoxication, falling, rising—all these are easily produced by the appropriate motions of the camera.

2) *Backward Motion*

We are still at an experimental stage in the use of such film devices as are of no particular advantage in a straightforward narrative film, but which because they are so radically divergent from nature should have great potentialities for the artist who does not wish slavishly to copy reality. Hitherto almost everything to which we have referred in the way of formal devices, from the choice of the camera angle to *montage,* is or can be used to give the spectator an image of the world as he knows it, even though it may be artistically selected and shaped. We shall now discuss certain artifices by means of which reality may be interpreted, but which do not result in images that are superficially realistic. With a revolving camera the spectator may be made to feel that if he were drunk he would see the world swaying in such a manner. But if he sees a shot in which people, motorcars, and everything move backward, all illusion of reality is lost. Since nowadays the film artist generally speaking is not allowed to carry his formative ideas beyond the point at which the average spectator might be prevented from thinking that he is watching "real" events, these admirable camera devices, which do not conform to realism, remain neglected.

Except for short humorous episodes in newsreels, little use has been found for backward motion. The potentialities are almost completely untried. For instance, in order to portray a particular manner in which a man enters a room, the director might take a backward motion shot of the actor walking backward out of the room—thus making him walk forward by reversing his walking backward. A hauntingly strange effect is likely to result. Moreover, tricks can be played on the force of gravity. I remember a scene somewhere in which an acrobat floated straight up in the air on the end of a parachute. The parachute gradually folded itself up into a compact little parcel, and the man swung neatly up into the airplane. It was backward motion, of course. Fragments joining up to form an unbroken pot; variations in facial expression shown backward—all these things have at most been tried occasionally as a joke, but have not yet been seriously used by artists. If one tries to visualize these possibilities, one gets an inkling of how very near we still are to the beginnings, and of how much we should lose if on economic or any other grounds the further evolution of film art were prevented.

It must be realized that the artistic film (that is, film which is produced without regard for the general public) will very soon reach a stage when quite exclusive films will be created, for which there will not be the smallest chance of popular success. Not that there will not always be plenty of naturalistic films; but in addition—if the businessmen will allow it— simply because the potentialities within an art medium create the urge to use them, whimsical, fantastic products will appear, compared with which the wildest futurism of the twenties will seem like innocuous ornaments.

3) *Accelerated Motion*

If a strip of negative is exposed in the camera at a slower speed than it is afterward projected, time appears compressed in the performance, the movement quickened. This accelerating effect has been used, for example, to express the speed of modern traffic— cars flash through the streets, people dash about in and out among each other in long snaky lines with astonishing suppleness and smoothness, and the leaves on the trees flap restlessly. This trick has occasionally been used by artists. Eisenstein, for instance, in *The General Line*, shows an office with the work going on appallingly slowly. Then suddenly someone crashes his fist on the table and raises Cain—and at once everything goes on at lightning speed. The clerks fly through the room, papers are signed and stamped as if by magic, and everything is finished off in a twinkling.

But acceleration can also be used for totally different purposes. In taking the shots for the I. G. Farben film *Miracle of Flowers,* which consisted of nothing but accelerated pictures of plants and is certainly the most fantastic, thrilling, and beautiful film ever made—in taking these shots it was shown that plants have expressive gestures, which we do not see because they are too slow for our minds but which become visible in accelerated pictures. The swaying, rhythmic breathing motions of the leaves, the excited dance of the leaves around the blossom, the almost voluptuous abandon with which the flower opens—the plants all at once come alive and show that they use expressive gestures exactly like those to which we are accustomed in men and animals. Watching a climbing plant anxiously groping, uncertainly seeking a hold, as its tendrils twine about a trellis, or a fading cactus bloom bowing its head and collapsing almost with a sigh, was an uncanny discovery of a new living world in a sphere in which one had of course always admitted life existed but had never been able to see it in action. Plants were suddenly and visibly enrolled in the ranks of living beings. One saw that the same principles applied to everything, the same code of behavior, the same difficulties, the same desires.

This of course was a lucky strike, and not much more is to be expected in this line. Nevertheless, it is always possible that equally exciting revelations may be in store concerning the behavior of inorganic matter. Occasional discoveries of this sort have already been made, as, for example, in the very curious accelerated films of the growth of crystals or of frost patterns on window panes.

Naturally such a device is usable for the artist. The Russians have shown how even completely abstract shots may be cut into quite naturalistic narrative films—such as the sudden gleam of a light or an indefinable, immaterial drizzle. These curious shots can, therefore, at least be used as stuff for montage. But why should not, even in the middle of a narrative film, a flower suddenly begin to wave its leaves wildly or put forth blossoms? (Jean Renoir's *The Little Match Girl* contains a picture in accelerated motion of roses bursting into bloom, though in this case there is no particular justification.)

4) *Slow Motion*

If the negative is exposed in the camera more rapidly than when the print is projected at the performance, the movement is slowed down to a fraction of the natural speed so that hundreds of frames are exposed in a second. This has hitherto been used almost exclusively in educational films in order to show the individual phases of rapid movements. In this way the technique of a boxer or of a violinist, the explosion of a bomb, the jump of a dog, can be analyzed closely. Slow motion has hardly been applied at all yet to artistic purposes, although it should be very useful. It might, for instance, serve to slow down natural movements grotesquely; but it can also create new movements, which do not appear as the retarding of natural movements but have a curious gliding, floating character of their own. Slow motion should be a wonderful medium for showing visions and ghosts.

Experiments ought to be made with slow motion just as with acceleration in order to find out how the expression of the human face and body appears when it is thus retarded and whether the result would not make for good montage material. What does a slow-motion picture of a face registering sudden terror or joy look like? Here again effects would be attainable which the spectator would not take for slowed-down versions of actually faster movements but accept as "originals" in their own right. (Apparently artists are experimenting with the use of slow motion. And once again Pudovkin is the pioneer. According to a newspaper report he is using slow motion in his new film *The World Is Beautiful* for such things as allowing a child's smile to develop slowly in a close-up.)

In *Entr'acte*, a surrealist film, a hearse is shown running away from the funeral procession. The hearse dashes through the streets and the mourners run after it in slow motion. Their legs are raised very slowly as though they clung to the ground and their arms swing backward and forward with ghastly deliberation. Here again, an irresistibly comic effect is achieved because one does not feel that one is seeing a retardation of normal running but a stylized take-off.

5) *Still Photographs*

Ordinary stationary photography is not as fundamentally remote from film as might be supposed. Still photographs may be used for other purposes besides the illustrated magazines and the showcases of movie palaces. A still photograph inserted in the middle of a moving film gives a very curious sensation; chiefly because the time character of the moving shots is carried over to the still picture, which therefore looks uncannily petrified. An ordinary photograph hardly ever gives an impression of rigid standstill because the dimension of motion is not applied to it, and the time spent looking at it is not considered as being the time that passes while the event shown in the picture takes place. But a still photograph cut into a film acts like the curse on Lot's wife. In the film *People on Sundays* (Film Studio 1929) a beach photographer is shown at work. Various people of whom he takes pictures appear, half-length, each first moving in the film, and then cut-in suddenly as "portrait." A smiling, naturally moving person is suddenly petrified as if touched by a magic wand, and persists for whole seconds in an oppressive immobility.

The particular effect produced by cutting-in a still picture cannot be made simply by the actor suddenly arresting a motion and holding it. Firstly, there is an astonishing difference between such voluntary cessation of motion and the absolute rigidity of a photograph; and, secondly, an actor can hardly hold the absurd momentary phases caught by a still photograph, which is not dependent upon the will of the actor and the laws of physical motion.

6) *Fading in, Fading out, Dissolving*

Sometimes in order to avoid sudden appearance a picture is allowed to grow slowly out of the darkness, or to disappear in the same way. Fading in and fading out can be used to show people's subjective perception;

for instance, when a person is waking up or falling asleep. But above all, it is a good means of keeping one scene distinct from the next; for since shots that follow immediately on one another usually appear as part of an unbroken time sequence, it is often not easy to show that an episode has come to an end, and that the scene of action is changing. If, however, the scene is faded out, the spectator feels that there is a break as though a curtain had dropped, and when something else fades in a new scene is expected.

Dissolving means the gradual transmuting of one shot into another. The two are not simply joined side by side by ordinary montage, but while the first shot becomes gradually fainter, the second begins indistinctly to appear, and by degrees gets stronger until it completely obliterates the first. Dissolving serves, like fading in and out, to mark a break between two scenes; it destroys the illusion of an unbroken passage of time and of one fixed place, because it presents a visible superimposition of times and places, and only separate things can be superimposed on one another, not things that follow one another in time or are immediately next to each other in space. Dissolving is a visible relative displacement of the coördinates of time (or space) and therefore impossible within a scene in which the unities of space and time are unbroken.

Dissolving often helps to heighten the effects of contrast and similarity in montage, for the more simply and easily one shot melts into another, the more striking it is if a connection of subject (similarity or contrast) between the two is suddenly noticed; and the more strongly is the connection emphasized. Two shots that are combined on the principle of similarity can be so dissolved into each other that the vague, indeterminate, neutral zone shows abstractly what is common to both shots: for instance, the "swinging" as such of a pendulum and of a playground swing.

7) *Superimposition, Simultaneous Montage*

From the dissolve there is only a step to showing several shots simultaneously. This has the same effect, but in a higher degree, as exposing the same plate twice over in ordinary photography. It is a good means of depicting confusion and chaos. Attempts have often been made to give the feeling of the medley and bustle of street traffic by showing various shots one on top of the other.

Quite other effects may, however, be achieved by this device. In the scene mentioned above from Feyder's *Les Nouveaux Messieurs,* the interplay of the orator and the mechanical piano is shown. Feyder superimposes a close-up of the speaker, gesticulating despairingly in the direction of the noise, upon a close-up of the drum inside the mechanical piano—the drumstick is seen moving up and down, and in the double picture it not only hits the drum but also the speaker's head. Thus the conflict that is only acoustic and narrative is transposed into the realm of the visual. And this has been done by artificially superimposing two episodes which in reality were taking place in the same space, but could not be brought into a visual association that would express the required connection. A certain aesthetic objection to the process is contained in the word "artificial."

The commotion of a dance has also been shown by

superimposition of dancers and the band. If these shots were simply put one after the other in ordinary montage it is fairly certain that they would make no more impression on the audience than simply indicating that the director wished to show that here is a band and here are people dancing. But superimposition is a simple way of showing the abstract substance of all of these scenes; that is, their meaning and mood rather than merely the events.

The method is convenient but somewhat artificial. This is obvious if it is compared with the effects of the selection of the camera angle which was discussed above. It was shown there how a particular connection between objects or events could be induced by optical juxtaposition or superimposition without interfering with reality, simply by a careful selection as regards kind and position of the objects in question, and then by choosing a camera angle which would make the required connection clear without the real spatial relationships in the scene being artificially changed or destroyed entirely. Example: the perspective superimposition of the convict and the prison bars. It must be admitted that in a naturalistic narrative film a superimposition by double exposure may easily give the impression of a foreign body, which interferes with the style of the rest; and, secondly, that the artistic effect of a scene is greater if it interprets and molds the material without doing violence to it. It is more striking, and more elegant. The abstract meaning which the artist brings into his production by the studied adaptation of visual devices should not appear as something external, arbitrarily introduced, but is much more effective if it is achieved simply by appropriate grouping and viewing of the material at hand. Multiple exposure is likely to give the feeling that the artist has achieved his effect too cheaply, and in too superficial a manner.

To be used and assessed in much the same way as superimposition is simultaneous montage—by which is meant montage of scenes juxtaposed within one image. Its first application was in the artistically suspect method by which memories and forebodings used to be shown: The hero is sitting deep in thought, and suddenly what he is thinking of appears as a circular insert in a corner at the top of the screen. This procedure is poor because the road from the idea to the visual form is too direct. "A man is thinking of his wife"—is primarily an abstract theme and difficult to render visibly unless it is in some way made concrete. A device may be adopted—the man may look at his wife's picture—and the situation is clear. Such a device is not original, but the abstract is thereby made sufficiently concrete. The artifice of simultaneous montage means an evasion of the effort to find an actual situation which will make the abstract part of the scene clear to the eyes of the audience without constraint. Two conceptually related items are simply placed side by side visually as well and thus a comprehensible pictorial representation of the theme is given—but by an artless, artificial method. Something of this kind has characterized most of the experiments that have been made with simultaneous montage. In Eisenstein's *The General Line,* where the vision of a gigantic stud bull suddenly appears over the cows, one has the feeling that—compared with his other inventions within the bounds of naturalistic style—the artist has made things too easy for himself, and in approaching the problem has considered the theme too much and the picture too little. It is true, however, that since the shot in question is definitely symbolic, there is less need of unifying it with the style of the rest.

Simultaneous montage is more impressive when it is meaningful not only in content but also in form. Thus Vertov has sometimes shown two or three images of the same scene on top of each other—the same machine, for instance, has driven across the screen three times—and from this a sort of symmetrical design has arisen which is not ineffective.

In the examples that have been discussed up to the present, simultaneous montage was so used that it could at once be recognized as such by the spectator, that is, so that the picture was bound to strike him as being a compound. Such amalgamations may, however, also be used to produce the illusion of a reality which does not exist. The same object may be present twice; a man may talk to himself. For this purpose separate shots are taken and are afterward so skillfully put together that it is impossible to detect the join. The device has enabled star players to shine in two parts at once. There was a great sensation when Henny Porten as a clumsy maidservant talked to Henny Porten the elegant lady—(Fancy! she can not only play any kind of a part, but she can do them all at once!) Artistic use of the wraith was made in Conrad Veidt's *The Student of Prague* and in Friedrich Ermler's *The Fragment of an Empire*. A symbolic battle scene occurs in the latter film: a German soldier and a Russian attack each other with bayonets. There is a sudden close-up—and it is seen that they both have the same face (both are being played by the same actor). They recognize each other and drop their bayonets. The generals in the German and Russian headquarters impotently rage, and order the renewal of the battle, but the officers to whom they give their orders again have the same face as the two soldiers. The folly of war that forces "Man" to turn on himself in a different uniform—the paradox has hardly ever been put quite so impressively. "All men have something in common, a certain kinship"—this abstract idea is made concrete by the creation of an artificial reality in which this common bond is made visible. Men all have the same face, and the fact that their uniforms are different seems futile and absurd in comparison with the surprisingly revealed visible truth.

8) *Special Lenses*

A multiplication of one and the same object can, apart from montage, also be achieved directly at the time the picture is shot by specially cut lenses, the insertion of prisms, and other means. Nevertheless the potentialities of these means do not seem to be very great. The same face may be multiplied a hundredfold, it may be distorted—but these are after all very special and rigid effects, which allow little variation and therefore must soon come to seem conventional and stale. Thus Granowsky in his *Song of Life* shows champagne glasses, infants, and skulls, in symbolic multiplication. This trick appears stereotyped, too mechanical, and easily degenerates into the ridiculous.

Charlie Chaplin managed to achieve unexpected and amusing effects by multiplying one man without the benefit of montage or special lenses in his mirror-labyrinth scene in *The Circus.*

9) *Manipulation of Focus*

In the old days any picture that was out of focus was simply considered a mistake. But as with so many other supposed shortcomings photography has learned to utilize it for particular purposes. At first the device was used, like fading in and out, to cause a picture to appear or disappear gradually. Sometimes it is the very uncertainty or incomprehensibility of the hazy picture that makes it attractive—it is impossible to guess what is coming, all kinds of speculations can be indulged in, and then suddenly the picture grows distinct, and everything is cleared up. In Eisenstein's *The General Line* the first appearance of the mysterious machine round which the plot revolves—the centrifugal milk separator—is made especially exciting, quite in accordance with the story, by the fact that the first close-up, which is to show the marvel clearly for the first time, begins out of focus. One sees a confused glittering of lights—the highlights on the polished aluminum surface of the machine, as is proved when the picture grows clear and the machine suddenly comes into focus as though out of a fog.

Moreover, indistinctness serves to give the subjective impression of hazy vision like that of a drunken man or someone awakening from anesthesia. It may even be used like a close-up to bring out details when the picture extends far into depth: since the range of focus of the camera is limited, the foreground and the background can be shown alternately by varying the focus, thus indicating, for example, a dialogue between someone standing near the front and someone farther back. The audience is compelled to look first at one figure, then the other, as the director chooses.

10) *Mirror Images*

Finally, instead of the real object, its image in some reflecting material may be photographed. This is especially effective if the spectator is not at first conscious of the trick, but supposes himself to be looking at a normal picture showing the actual object. For instance, a photograph might be taken of the reflection of a man in an absolutely still sheet of water; and since the spectator could neither tell that the camera had been turned upside down nor that he was looking at a reflection instead of the reality, he might believe he was seeing a normal picture. Then the water might suddenly become agitated; the picture would waver, be distorted, become unrecognizable. Such a scene might be used, even if no water occurred in the film, simply as a means of showing the dissolution of a man of flesh and blood into a quavering caricature, or to depict hallucinations (cf. the dream images in Granowsky's *Song of Life*).

The object might also be photographed in a looking glass. The spectator thinks he is watching the physical objects themselves, he follows the plot, and suddenly a stone is hurled into the picture, the glass is splintered; reality—as far as the spectator is concerned—is shattered. It would result in a very powerful visual shock.

In the same way all kinds of distorting mirrors can be used; and again, if the device is applied at all skillfully, the spectator will not at first notice that it is only a mirror that has been photographed, and will therefore accept the distortion as the real thing.

SUMMARY OF THE FORMATIVE MEANS OF CAMERA AND FILM STRIP

Challenged by the favorite argument of people who dislike film—that it is nothing but the mechanical reproduction of nature and therefore not art—we have examined in detail the various aspects of filmic representation and have found that even at the most elementary level there are significant divergences between the image that the camera makes of reality and that which the human eye sees. We found, moreover, that such differences not only exist, but that they can be used to mold reality for artistic purposes. In other words, that what might be called the "drawbacks" of film technique (and which engineers are doing their best to "overcome") actually form the tools of the creative artist.

For the sake of emphasis and clearness, a short summary of the characteristics of the film medium and their application is appended.

1. EVERY OBJECT MUST BE PHOTOGRAPHED FROM ONE PARTICULAR VIEWPOINT.

   Applications.

   a) View that shows the shape of the object most characteristically.

   b) View that conveys a particular conception of the object (e.g., worm's-eye view, indicating weight and forcefulness).

    c) View that attracts the spectator's attention by being unusual.

    d) Surprise effect due to the concealment of the back side (Chaplin sobbing; no!—mixing a cocktail!)

2. OBJECTS ARE PUT BEHIND OR BESIDE ONE ANOTHER BY PERSPECTIVE.

  Applications.

    a) Unimportant objects are hidden by being wholly or partly covered; important objects are thereby emphasized.

    b) Surprise effect by the sudden revealing of what had been concealed by something else.

    c) Optical swallowing-up—one object comes in front of another and obliterates it.

    d) Relationships indicated by perspective connections (convict and prison bars).

    e) Decorative surface patterns.

3. APPARENT SIZE. OBJECTS NEAR THE FRONT ARE LARGE, AND THOSE BEHIND SMALL.

  Applications.

    a) Emphasizing of individual parts of an object (feet thrust toward the camera come out huge).

    b) Increase and decrease of size to indicate relative power.

4. ARRANGEMENT OF LIGHT AND SHADE. ABSENCE OF COLOR.

  Applications.

    a) Molding the volume and relief of the object at will by the placing of lights and shadows.

    b) Accentuating, grouping, segregating, hiding by the arrangement of light and shade.

5. DELIMITATION OF THE SIZE OF THE IMAGE.
   Applications.
   - *a*) Selection of the theme of the picture.
   - *b*) Showing the whole or a part.
   - *c*) Surprise effect. Some object, which was always present but had been cut off by the frame, suddenly comes into the picture from outside.
   - *d*) Increase of suspense; the center of interest lies outside the picture (for example, only the effect of it on someone is seen).

6. DISTANCE FROM THE OBJECT IS VARIABLE.
   Applications.
   - *a*) Objects can be made small or large.
   - *b*) Choice of optimal distance (a pin, a mountain).
   - *c*) Relativization of dimensions (doll's house— human house).

7. ABSENCE OF SPACE-TIME CONTINUUM.
   Applications: Montage.
   - *a*) Showing beside (and among) one another, episodes that are separate in time.
   - *b*) Juxtaposition of places that are actually separate.
   - *c*) Presenting the characteristic features of a scene by showing selected portions of it.
   - *d*) Combination of things whose connection is not one of time and space but of meaning (symbolic) or shape.
   - *e*) Imperceptible montage. Illusion of altered (fantastic) reality (sudden appearances and disappearances, etc.).
   - *f*) Rhythm of the sequence of shots by "short" or "long" montage, etc.

8. Absence of Spatial Orientation.
   Applications.
   a) Relativization of movement: static things move, or moving things stand still.
   b) Relativization of spatial coördinates (vertical, horizontal, etc.).

9. Lessening of Depth Perception.
   Applications.
   a) Perspective alterations of size (cf. point 3) made more compelling.
   b) Perspective connections in the plane projection (cf. point 2) made more compelling.

10. Absence of Sound.
    Applications.
    a) Stronger emphasis on what is visible; as, for instance, on facial expression and gesture.
    b) Qualities and effects of unheard sounds specially brought out by their being transposed into the sphere of the visible (suddenness of revolver shot—birds rising).

11. The Camera Is Mobile.
    Applications.
    a) Representation of subjective states such as falling, rising, swaying, staggering, giddiness, etc.
    b) Representation of subjective attitudes such as the individual being always the center of the scene (i.e., of the plot).

12. The Film Can Run Backward.
    Applications.
    a) Reversal of the direction of movements.
    b) Reversal of events (fragments join to make a whole object).

13. ACCELERATION.

Applications.

a) Visible acceleration of a movement or an event; change in the dynamic character (to symbolize bustle).

b) Compression of time (the breathing of flowers).

14. SLOW MOTION.

Applications.

a) Visible retarding of a movement or an event; change in dynamic character (laziness, gliding).

b) Lengthening of periods of time (showing more clearly events that pass very rapidly).

15. INTERPOLATION OF STILL PHOTOGRAPHS.

Applications.

Sudden stopping of movement; paralysis (Lot's wife).

16. FADING IN AND OUT, DISSOLVING.

Applications.

a) To mark breaks in the action.

b) Subjective impressions: waking up, falling asleep.

c) Stronger contact and coherence between two pictures by dissolving one into the other.

17. SUPERIMPOSITION (MULTIPLE EXPOSURE).

Applications.

a) Chaos, confusion.

b) Indication of relationships by juxtaposition and superimposition.

c) Indication of symbolic similarities.

d) Modifications of reality (wraiths).

18. SPECIAL LENSES.

Applications.
Multiplication, distortion.
19. MANIPULATION OF FOCUS.
Applications.
   a) Subjective impressions: waking up, going to sleep.
   b) Suspense by gradual exposition ("appears slowly").
   c) Directing the spectator's gaze to the back or the foreground.
20. MIRROR IMAGES.
Applications.
Destroying, distorting an object (or the "world").

Even without going into the question of what the camera photographs—that is, what objects are selected, what sort of events and setting, how the actors are made up, and so forth—we have seen what unlimited possibilities of molding and transforming nature are contained in the properties of the film medium itself. The film artist chooses a particular scene that he wishes to photograph. Within this scene he can leave out objects, cover them up, make them prominent, and yet not interfere with reality. He can increase or decrease the size of things, can make small objects larger than big ones, and vice versa.

He can put beside, behind, among one another, things that are entirely separate in space and time. He can pick out what is important, however small and inconspicuous it may be, and thus let the part represent the whole. He can lay down what is upright, and set upright what is recumbent, can move what stands still, and arrest what is moving. He eliminates entire areas of sensory perception, and thereby brings others into higher relief, ingeniously making them take the place of those that are missing. He can let the dumb speak and thereby interpret the sphere of sound.

He shows the world not only as it appears objectively but also subjectively. He creates new realities, in which things can be multiplied, turns their movements and actions backward, distorts them, retards or accelerates them. He calls into existence magical worlds where the force of gravity disappears, mysterious powers move inanimate objects, and broken things are made whole. He brings into being symbolic bridges between events and objects that have had no connection in reality. He intervenes in the structure of nature to make quivering, disintegrate ghosts of concrete bodies and spaces. He arrests the progress of the world and of things, and changes them to stone. He breathes life into stone and bids it move. Of chaotic and illimitable space he creates pictures beautiful in form and of profound significance, as subjective and complex as painting.

It must be admitted that most film directors do not make much original use of the artistic means at their disposal. They do not produce works of art but tell the people stories. They and their employers and audiences are not concerned with form but with content. Nevertheless there are plenty of examples to show that film is capable of better things; not a great many first-rate works of art, complete, coherent, and highly finished—the art is still too young for that, it is still too much in the experimental stage—but there are nevertheless enough films that show in individual scenes, individual inventions, in the efforts of individual actors, what might be, what still lies hidden and untapped. And there is, in art, nothing to prevent one's clinging to the little that is good, instead of the great quantity that is bad.

3 The Content of the Film

THE MIND THROUGH THE BODY

The raw material that the film can use for its representations consists entirely of material objects and physical happenings. But mental processes may be expressed by means of these. There are, above all, the play of the human face and the gestures of the body and limbs—by means of them human thought and feeling are expressed in the most direct and familiar way. These are, however, not the only means of making inner happenings externally visible, and perhaps not even the best and most effective.

Since most people are not in the habit of observing their fellow men in everyday life to see how far their gestures are vivid and significant, it seldom occurs to them how unnatural and exaggerated are those of most film actors. The "natural acting" of everyday life is curious. It is most ambiguous and indeterminate, enigmatic and individual. Many people are sparing of it, and its use is monotonous, being confined to a very few muscles. A man's facial expression often does not seem to the average beholder in the least indicative of his mental state. Some people look as if they were laughing when they are crying, and some people's smiles are very acid. And, above all, much everyday expression fails to convey a well-defined meaning: it is not striking, one does not know how to interpret it, it may mean resignation or doubt or stupidity or reserve. The face is contorted and full of wrinkles, but the whole effect is not quite harmonious, it does not convey a homogeneous message. Much facial expression is comprehensibile only because it is a part of a situation, because the conversation and various other indications reveal what the man is feeling. It is only in this way that the untidy play of lines in his face is understood as meaning embarrassment or greed or pleasure.

The expression of animals and primitive peoples, though for reasons of our own upbringing difficult for us to understand, is intrinsically much more distinct. That it has degenerated to such an extent in civilized man is due to several causes. All our social customs tend to the impoverishment of external expression because it is considered improper in human intercourse to manifest personal desires and feelings unrestrainedly. If one observes a mother with her child, one notices her to systematically break the child of its natural gesture of face and limbs ("Don't stare at the gentleman like that!"—"Sit still!") Again, modern man is not so direct in his thoughts and feelings as primitive man and the animals. The variety of his motives, the suppleness and flexibility of thought, the lightning rapidity of the clash of tiny impulses and repressions, all have their natural echo in the play of features and in gestures; and so has the fact that this variety of stirrings often is not integrated in a clear-cut whole.

In a good work of art, however, everything must be clear—if anything indistinct is to be shown, it must be distinctly indistinct—and therefore human expression on the screen must be plain and unmistakable.

Hence a film actor must be capable of producing "pure" expression. His face, for example, must be so constituted that the required expression emerges quite clearly down to the smallest details. That an actor does not "get across," is often because he cannot make each individual muscle fit in with what is required. He may have an indefinite, weak mouth, which refuses to stiffen up with the rest of the face when he is supposed to register strong-mindedness; or a nervous tension of the eyebrows, which he cannot relax even when the face is supposed to be expressing placid cheerfulness.

Why does the "pure" acting of the movies not seem unnatural to the audience, who, after all, are accustomed in real life to people whose expression is more or less indistinct? Most people's perception in these matters is, as I said, not very acute. They are not in the habit of observing closely the play of features of their fellow men—either in real life or at the movies. They are satisfied with grasping the meaning of what they see. Thus, in fact, they often take in the overemphasized—sometimes highly conventional and unnatural—expression of film actors more easily than any that is too naturalistic. And as far as lovers of art are concerned, they do not look at the movies for imitations of nature but for art. They know that artistic representation is always explaining, refining, making clear the object depicted. Things that in real life are imperfectly realized, merely hinted at, and entangled with other things appear in a work of art complete, entire and clearly, free from extraneous matters. This is also true of acting in film.

The stylizing of acting must, nevertheless, remain within strict limits. In a narrative film, that is, a "naturalistic" film, a point is soon reached at which the shaping of expression turns into crude artificiality. It is, of course, understandable that a medium so strongly dependent upon the visible—particularly in the case of the silent film—will easily induce the actor and the director to give strong prominence to facial expression and gesture. Slapstick shows with especial clearness how very suitable to film is this exaggerated play of feature and limb. But in "naturalistic" film care must be exercised. Any artistic medium tempts the artist to do violence to nature; and although it is fitting for the artist to submit to the conditions of his medium, it is on the other hand essential that he should not let himself be led into being unfaithful to nature.

The average movie actor has developed a technique of expression to which the spectator easily grows accustomed because it is in a certain sense very "filmic." It must, nevertheless, be rejected as inartistic, especially since it also serves as a cheap trick to translate any desired mental state into a language of visual stereotypes. When the actor's chest heaves visibly, it is clear to everyone that agitation is intended. This up-and-down movement is also pictorially very satisfactory and effective, but the outrage to nature is usually too violent for such an interpretation to be admitted as "natural." The acting is not only unpleasantly amplified, but every thought, every emotion is simply translated into the visible, regardless of the fact that by no means everything a man thinks and feels is obvious in his face and gestures. A language of signs has been developed which is already nearly as void as if instead a title were inserted to this effect: "Erwin is terribly upset by this news." Certainly sound film by the introduction of speech appears to beneficially reduce this function of acting.

Meanwhile, however, good actors and directors have shown that the best effects are almost always achieved by "acting" as little as possible. The great actors work with very slight expenditure of muscular energy, they achieve a substantial effect by their very presence. Stage actors, who are obliged on account of the poor optical conditions of the theater to play everything with overstatement, are accustomed to exaggerated effects. This technique, however, soon proved to be unsuitable and superfluous for film use, since the most insignificant gesture can be seen quite clearly owing to the enormous enlargement of the picture when it is thrown on the screen. The development—especially under Russian influence—has been toward an increased restriction of the play of feature and toward using the actor as one of the "properties" chosen for his typicalness and allowed to make his effect simply by his presence, by being introduced in the proper context. For this of course a well-constructed script is necessary. If the actor does not "act," his mental state must be made perfectly clear at every moment by what is going on around him—even if he is doing nothing but staring straight ahead. This development may possibly lead to the employment of fewer actors and an increasing number of chance comers who happen to be the right type—as has already happened in Russia. For if the film continues to develop a style that reduces the contribution of acting by expressing meaning through photogenic narration (in the script) and the devices of the camera, man will eventually be one "prop" among many, and like a dog or a teapot be required to furnish little but his appearance and presence. For this purpose "real" types are better than make-believe; a real insurance salesman, policeman, cobbler, furniture mover, better than extras made up to look like them—that is unquestionable. The actor is only necessary when "acting" is required; hence amateurs, real types, are useless for the theater.

It will be obvious from this that "acting" is not the only means of expressing mental states in a film. (It is proposed to leave aside the expressive value of the spoken word here, especially as nearly all that can be said about it applies not only to talkies but also to the theater.) And that is very important, for if film were dependent upon such acting for the expression of human striving, the expression of the body would soon be blunted as an instrument—it would still be understood, but the audience would no longer be moved by it. It may be reasonable to assert that an actor can never achieve the same depth of artistry in a silent film as on the stage for the material at his disposal—the mere expression of face and gesture without the interpretation of spoken words—is too primitive. If an actor has to declaim one of Shakespeare's great monologues, he has every opportunity of making it into a great artistic achievement all by himself. But it would be unfair to expect him to rise to equally great heights if he were allowed to use nothing but silent play. A silent film may be as profound as a Shakespearian drama; but the "dumb action" of a player can never be as profound as Hamlet's monologue.

It will be understood that I am arguing not against the silent film but against film relying heavily upon silent "acting" in the conventional sense. What other means, then, are available by which mental states may be represented? Here is an elementary example: Everyone knows that favorite theme, the tragic clown, such as the one in Sjöström's *He Who Gets Slapped,* where a scientist who has fallen on bad times becomes a clown. His face has been painted into a thick chalky horror. Nothing of the actor's face can be seen through this mask, and yet the spectator feels most vividly the agony of the humiliated creature simply because he knows what the man was like before, and hence what he must be feeling now. Without the actor's assisting in any way, the state of mind of the figure which he embodies is thus clearly realized by everyone; for the plot of the whole film is so constructed that the psychology of this scene is unmistakable. A similar example is Professor Unrath in *The Blue Angel.*

In this way the role of the actor may be reduced to his simply appearing. But the actor can also express mental states by what he does, and yet abandon "expressive" acting almost entirely. De Mille's film *Chicago* contains shots of the public galleries in a law court where a sensational case is being tried. There is a close-up of a bench full of girls who are following the case absorbedly with wide-open eyes, and at the same time chewing gum—their mouths working like machinery. Then comes an exciting point in the case, and again a close-up of the girls is shown, and suddenly, as if at the word of command, they all stop chewing, showing their mental state: excitement—they hold their breath. Excitement may also be indicated purely by facial expression, but it is more arresting to see a mental state reflected by such an original element of action. The staring eyes and heaving breasts have been seen hundreds of times and can no longer make the spectator actually realize "excitement." But this indirect method of showing it is so fresh that it helps to make the mental state most evident. It is striking because the connection between the external event and the internal emotion is not only conceptual and thematic but profits from a structural similarity between the two. The visible event—a regular rhythmical movement suddenly stopped dead—also contains the most marked characteristic of the inward process: a sudden interruption of the calm interest with which the girls had been following the case. And this is cleverly translated into the sphere of the visible.

Thus an external event, some little piece of action, is invented which reflects the mental state of the actor. When, in *The Woman in the Moon,* Willy Fritsch with his paper shears cuts the heads off the flowers standing in a vase on his desk while he is telephoning, his gesture shows much more clearly than his facial expression how agitated he is. Moreover it is real film stuff (even though elementary) because it is action, visible action. In Feyder's *Les Nouveaux Messieurs* is a scene where the old Count is telling his friend, the dancer, that the Minister Gaillac has been transferred to a post abroad. Gaillac is secretly Suzanne's lover. She is therefore very much upset by the news but must keep a tight hold on herself and make no sign. How is this done? Suzanne and the Count are having tea. He tells her the news as she is pouring. She does not move a muscle of her face and says politely: "Really?" But her hand grows unsteady, and she spills the tea into the saucer. There was hardly a way of expressing Suzanne's feelings facially, for the point of the scene was that she was obliged to suppress her feelings. Even so, a less capable director, unable to think of a way of circumventing the difficulty in a "filmic" way, would not have hesitated to let the girl act out her shock: start, turn away, look nervously out of the corners of her eyes—and leave the old Count to pretend he noticed nothing. Jacques Feyder, on the contrary, introduces the small episode that enables him to show Suzanne's repressed demeanor and her real feelings at the same time, and this without doing violence to reality. Examples such as these show best what good film work is.

In this connection Greta Garbo's famous love scene, the cigarette scene in *Flesh and the Devil,* may be recalled. She has met the young officer John Gilbert at a party. They have already danced together very absorbedly, gazing into each other's eyes; but externally everything is still quite conventional—two people who were indifferent to each other might do just the same. Nothing has yet been acknowledged, they only have glimmerings of what might be . . . They go into the garden, the girl takes a cigarette between her lips, the man lights a match, but instead of lighting up, she makes a tiny retreating movement, the flame illumines the two faces, they look at each other. This sudden arbitrary interruption of the social ritual explains their change of attitude better than any explicit acting out of feelings; it is enough. Something different is going to happen.

In film inanimate properties are just as useful as the human actor to show psychic states. A broken windowpane may be as good as a quivering mouth, a heap of dead cigarette stubs as the nervous drumming of fingers. Once again the classification—so characteristic of film—of man as one among many objects is plainly revealed. The traces of human strivings are as visible on inanimate objects as they are on the body itself.

MEANING AND INVENTION

It is often said that silent films convey no ideas and that indeed it is impossible that they should because language plays too small a part in them. Now if by ideas we mean abstractly formulated thoughts, film will not in fact provide them. But this kind of intellectual content does not play a very great part even in literature—the art of words par excellence. In literature language is often used simply to describe concrete events—to say what the characters in a story are doing and thinking, what the surroundings are like; and if the people talk, their conversation generally turns on very concrete matters. It is not the worst kind of literature in which language is used for description and not for abstract reflections. In this matter, then, there is no essential difference between literature and film. Literature uses words for description; film, pictures. In both media the guiding ideas are not given in abstract form but clothed in concrete episodes.

That films need not lack depth has been proved in many masterpieces. Chaplin's *The Gold Rush* affords memorable examples. There is the scene where Charlie as a starving prospector cooks and eats his dirty oiled boots. Elegantly and with perfect table manners he carves his unusual dish—he lifts off the upper so that the sole with the nails sticking up in it is left like the backbone of a fish from which the meat has been removed; he carefully sucks the nails as if they were chicken bones, and winds the laces round the fork like spaghetti.

In this scene the contrast between rich and poor is symbolized in an incomparably original, striking, and graphic manner. The same contrast may be made in a film, as has often been done, by showing the scanty meal of a poor man side by side with the luxurious fare of a rich man. Such an effect, however, is taken directly from the abstract, is conventional, unoriginal, and therefore tends to lose its appeal and to become artistically worthless.

If the scene in *The Gold Rush* showed nothing but a starving man wolfing a cooked boot, it would be no more than a grotesque caricature of poverty. The excellence and forcibleness of the scene consists in the fact that in depicting misery the contrast of riches is given simultaneously by the most original and visually striking similarity of this meal to that of a rich man.

$$\text{Carcass of the boot} = \text{carcass of a fish}$$
$$\text{Nails} = \text{chicken bones}$$
$$\text{Bootlaces} = \text{spaghetti}$$

Chaplin makes the contrast painfully clear to the eyes of the spectator by demonstrating the similarity of form of such objectively different things. And the great artistry of the invention lies in that such an elemental, profoundly human theme as "hunger versus good living" is presented pictorially by objective means that are so truly filmic. Nothing more purely visual can be conceived than such association of the shapes of things.

By eating the most wretched food imaginable as if it were a choice dish, and with suitably elegant manners, Chaplin not only shows poverty as such, but (so to speak) poverty as a low grade of wealth, as a distortion of good living. And by creating this relationship he makes misery seem doubly miserable— since smallness is made small by largeness, and blackness black by whiteness.

Quite in general, what distinguishes Charlie Chaplin is that he is not only the ragged vagabond but he is the destitute person shown in the perspective of the wealthy. His jaunty bowler hat, his coat vaguely resembling a dinner jacket, his dandified little stick and mustache describe poverty as the lack of riches. This is much more striking than unrelated "raggedness."

Another scene in *The Gold Rush* which was invented on the same principle as the boot dinner is the one where the big gold miner, half-crazed with hunger, suddenly sees his mate Charlie as a fowl and tries to catch him and eat him. Charlie's helpless gesticulations turn into the flapping of wings, and when he leans over the stove the chicken seems to be bending down to drink. The climax of the craving for food, when man lays violent hands on man, when the friend's body becomes edible flesh—a deep-seated feature of the human mind—is again made pictorial by an unexpected resemblance, this time between the appearance of the friend and a fine fat chicken. And once again it is the visual similarity of intrinsically opposite things that expresses the dramatic contradiction.

One more example from *The Gold Rush*: Charlie has attained the height of his desires—he is dancing with the girl he adores. But his trousers are slipping, and he seizes a rope and ties it round his waist. A large dog is tied to the other end of the rope and has to join in the dance. Thus, even when he achieves happiness and success, the ballast of bad luck is tied to him.

Two examples from Chaplin's *A Woman of Paris*: a girl brings another the exciting news that her lover is unfaithful to her. The friend is being massaged and, while the two girls are discussing the matter with great emotion, the masseuse is seen carrying on her work dully and unmoved; she swings backward and forward in time with her hands as calmly as the pendulum of a clock; and quite mechanically without betraying any interest she keeps looking first at one and then at the other of the two excited girls. This robot-like indifference which—in true film fashion—is depicted not only by the expression on her face but by the unruffled backward and forward movement of her body, brings the perturbation of the two main figures into high relief. The fact that the world rolls on quietly and inevitably even though certain individuals are desperate is very strikingly symbolized by a particular event.

A similar theme, though differently depicted, is in Pudovkin's *The End of St. Petersburg*. Two peasants are on their way to the city. This is their last hope—they have nothing more to eat. Struggling on in silent despair against the wind they cross field after field. Then a windmill is shown, its vanes revolving calmly and indifferently. Pudovkin has flashed this picture into that of the two peasants several times—it symbolizes the world moving steadily on, and serves as a contrasting foil to the dramatic action.

The final scene in *A Woman of Paris*: The man and woman, Adolphe Menjou and Edna Purviance, have parted. She now lives in the country. One day she is driving along the road in a cart with her pupils, when her former lover comes from the other direction in a fine car. The vehicles pass without the occupants recognizing each other, the motorcar vanishes in the distance—it is the end of the film. Here again the abstract fact has been transposed with absolute faithfulness into concrete form: the paths of two lives cross and separate. But the concrete episode which is chosen to show it is not conventional or trite, it is very original; the superimposition of two congruent things—the path of life and the country road—is brilliant and arresting.

If one examines Chaplin's development, one finds that the human quality of his humorous inventions grows increasingly profound. The first two-reelers, which are hardly distinguishable from those of other artists of the same period, consist of inventions that are pure jokes, with little or no serious background. They are also brilliant and amusing, but are not to be compared with films like *The Gold Rush,* in which the profound sadness of the jesting brings tears to the eyes.

Even in the first shorts the inventions often rest upon the principle that unexpected associations are created between very divergent objects. Charlie as assistant to a pawnbroker examines the alarm clock brought in by a customer as if he were a doctor examining a patient. He puts a stethoscope to his ears and listens to the clock ticking (heartbeat—clockwork), then percusses it with a hammer, most carefully and with a deadly serious face, takes off the back with a can opener (food can—alarm clock), pulls the wheels and springs out with a pair of tweezers, and eventually throws the whole pile of oddments into the unhappy owner's hat saying that the clock is no use to him. This scene is very comic but essentially unenlightening, unless one wishes to maintain, as one critic did, that an amusing parallel with psychoanalysis is suggested. Unexpected likeness of form or function is used, but there is no sort of inherent connection between the things that are so joined—there is no deeper meaning to the idea of equating a food can and an alarm clock, a heartbeat and the ticking of a clock. The fact that these things are objectively so far apart, but are so ingeniously brought together, is the whole substance of such a "gag."

This principle of demonstrating unexpected formal

similarities in things objectively quite unconnected is also used frequently in other forms of art. The aesthetic attraction of rhyme as of alliteration is due to the stress laid on the formal similarity of words that are not similar in their meanings. (It may be possible by such an explanation to derive rhyme and alliteration from the same aesthetic principle.) Novelists use the same device in inventing telling episodes. No doubt there is something similar in music. It would be interesting to investigate these connections more closely.

On the other hand there are relations to the psychology of productive thinking. A sudden change in the functions of an object or episode is found as often in comic films as in processes of thought, and in these as often as in jokes. For example—Charlie Chaplin as a policeman. The burly gangster in order to frighten the little man bends a gas lamp as if it were a piece of wire. Charlie grasps the lamp and pulls it down a little farther until the big man's head is covered by the glass shade—gas pours into the shade and the "heavy" is overcome by it. The function of the gas lamp has thus been "restructured." At first, its psychological character is merely that of a strong pole, something that can be bent to attest one's strength. The shade, in itself merely a protection for the incandescent mantle, suddenly and unexpectedly turns into a container for a head. The gas, hitherto used only for illumination, is suddenly turned into a weapon, and the bending of the lamp pole, which was primarily nothing but the consequence of a trial of strength, becomes the condition that is necessary to apply the medical procedure of anesthetizing a man with gas.

The same processes frequently take place when someone has a "good idea" or suddenly understands something. The psychologist Köhler has shown this by experiments in animal psychology: when chimpanzees suddenly realize, for example, that some wooden boxes lying about their cage can be used to erect a structure to help them climb up to the fruit which is hanging at the top of the cage. Here too an object changes its function in an unexpected manner. (Cf. here Max Wertheimer's work on productive thinking.)

And finally, when the naked man whom the deceived husband finds in the bedroom closet answers the question as to what he is doing there in the famous words: "You won't believe me, but I'm waiting for a bus!" an episode ("a man stands waiting") is also suddenly and unexpectedly restructured. Except that in a joke, as in a comic film, the effect is amusing chiefly because there is no meaningful connection between the two externally similar features, but in a "good idea" (the apes') the restructuring makes for success and enlightenment.

Chaplin's inventions are thoroughly "filmic" but usable not only in film. In the music-hall turns of the clown Grock, for instance, there were gags that would not be out of place in a Chaplin film. They were based entirely on optical principles—as when Grock suddenly used as a slide the lid of the piano, which he had lifted off and set standing up against the instrument. Here too is a definite restructuring: a slope is made out of the lid leaning up against the grand piano—primarily nothing more than a superfluous part that has been laid aside. The purely accidental and irrelevant fact of its oblique position becomes a usable attribute. Chaplin's pantomimic tricks are applicable not only to the film but also to the theater stage (his career began on the music-hall stage) because the early American film comedies represent a film style before the "discovery" of the camera and montage. In these early films, camera and montage serve mainly as technical recording devices for what is acted out on the scene, and are therefore unessential.

In Eisenstein's *The General Line* a tractor is seen crashing through the fences that cut up a field into a number of small holdings. The scene is intended to convey symbolically that the tractor, the emblem of modern agriculture, enforces collectivism. This idea is, however, not of a very high grade artistically because the episode that is shown simply makes a concrete scene of an abstract notion, regardless of whether it is likely to occur in reality. In a "naturalistic" film any symbolic scene must be so planned that it not only makes this implicit meaning visible in a comprehensible manner, but also fits smoothly into the action and the world depicted in the film. For the unexpected and gripping effect is produced mainly by disclosing the congruence of two themes which are fraught with meaning inherently and independently of each other. In the Eisenstein example, one of the two themes (the concrete) is sacrificed to the other (the symbolized thought), and the congruence is achieved artificially. There is something contrived about using a tractor to crash the fences. The scene

is reminiscent of Ermler's *The Fragment of an Empire,*
in which a tank runs over a crucifix to which a terrified soldier is clinging—although since this scene
makes no pretense at reality, it cannot be attacked on
the score of artificiality.

On the other hand, the effect is excellent when, in
the same Eisenstein film, a bureaucratic Soviet official
cleans his pen on the china head of Lenin that adorns
his inkpot. Here we have the underlying idea—
"bureaucrats smirch the ideal of the revolution"—
made concrete without any interference with the
natural progress of events. The most common symbol
of the revolution—Lenin—is brought into the same
picture and the same action with the official in an un-
contrived manner, and the smirching is very naturally
motivated in the concrete event.

In contrast to this is another scene from *A Woman of
Paris:* The girl implores her lover to marry her, as she
is longing for a regular married life and children. The
lover—to put an end to the tiresome discussion—steps
over to the window and looks out. He sees a fat
woman, cross and worn-out by a family of naughty
children; smiling, he draws the girl toward the window and points out the group. Though amusing, this
is not a particularly clever invention, because the
abstract idea, which has to be made concrete and
brought into the scene ("drawbacks to married life"),
is rather too obviously "dragged in." The fat woman
has no connection with the main plot, her appearance
is purely symbolic, a mere coincidence without inherent motivation. And such coincidences are out of
place in a work of art.

Invention is by no means used only to express

abstract ideas in film. Often the clever devices are simply intended to depict a factual part of the narrative aptly and impressively. For example: a girl has had a baby that she would like to be rid of. The picture shows first the mother standing outside the front door of an apartment (so that the door is more or less concealed); the door opens; a stout woman admits the visitor; the door is closed and now the nameplate is seen: "Mrs. Jones. Midwife." This is not a particularly brilliant invention, but it gives an idea of the technique by which things are made clear that would otherwise not be obvious from the pictured episode. Who is the woman whom the girl has gone to see? The nameplate lies naturally in the course of the narrative. A clever touch is the moment's tension that is achieved by not giving the explanation until the episode has passed and the door is shut again.

Finally, the meaning of a film scene that goes beyond mere narration need not always be an abstractly formulable idea. In *The General Line* the peasant woman comes to the fat kulak and lays her petition before him. He sits up on his couch, picks up a ladle, takes a large spoonful out of a huge bowl of punch, drinks it, then speaks, refusing the request, and sinks lazily back onto his pillow. While he is dropping back, a close-up is shown of the ladle dropping into the bowl, with a very similar slapping motion. The parallel that is here drawn introduces no abstract idea. The visual essence, so to speak, of the main action is simply repeated as a sort of metaphoric echo in a different material and therefore made particularly emphatic.

4 *The Complete Film*

The technical development of the motion picture will soon carry the mechanical imitation of nature to an extreme. The addition of sound was the first obvious step in this direction. The introduction of sound film must be considered as the imposition of a technical novelty that did not lie on the path the best film artists were pursuing. They were engaged in working out an explicit and pure style of silent film, using its restrictions to transform the peep show into an art. The introduction of sound film smashed many of the forms that the film artists were using in favor of the inartistic demand for the greatest possible "naturalness" (in the most superficial sense of the word). By sheer good luck, sound film is not only destructive but also offers artistic potentialities of its own. Owing to this accident alone the majority of art-lovers still do not realize the pitfalls in the road pursued by the movie producers. They do not see that the film is on its way to the victory of wax museum ideals over creative art.

The development of the silent film was arrested possibly forever when it had hardly begun to produce good results; but it has left us with a few splendidly mature films. In the future, no doubt, "progress" will be faster. We shall have color films and stereoscopic films, and the artistic potentialities of the sound film will be crushed at an even earlier stage of their development.

What will the color film have to offer when it reaches

technical perfection? We know what we shall lose artistically by abandoning the black-and-white film. Will color ever allow us to achieve a similar compositional precision, a similar independence of "reality"?

The masterpieces of painting prove that color provides wider possibilities than black-and-white and at the same time permits of a very exact and genuine style. But can painting and color photography be compared? Whereas the painter has a perfectly free hand with color and form in presenting nature, photography is obliged to record mechanically the light values of physical reality. In achromatic photography the reduction of everything to the gray scale resulted in an art medium that was sufficiently independent and divergent from nature. There is not much likelihood of any such transposition of reality into a qualitatively different range of colors in color film. To be sure, one can eliminate individual colors—one may, for example, cut out all blues, or, vice versa, one may cut out everything except the blues. Probably it is possible also to change one or more color tones qualitatively—for example, give all reds a cast of orange or make all the yellows greenish—or let colors change places with one another—turn all blues to red and all reds to blue—but all this would be, so to speak, only transposition of reality, mechanical shifts, whose usefulness as a formative medium may be doubted. Hence there remains only the possibility of controlling the color by clever choice of what is to be photographed. All kinds of fine procedures are conceivable, especially in the montage of colored pictures, but it must not be overlooked that in this way the subjective formative virtues of the camera, which are so distinctive a characteristic of film, will be more and more restricted, and the artistic part of the work will be more and more focused upon what is set up and enacted *before* the camera. The camera is thereby increasingly relegated to the position of a mere mechanical recording machine.

Above all, it is hardly realistic to speculate on the artistic possibilities of the color film without keeping in mind that at the same time we are likely to be presented with the three-dimensional film and the wide screen. Efforts in these directions are in progress. The illusion of reality will thereby have been increased to such a degree that the spectator will not be able to appreciate certain artistic color effects even if they should be feasible technically. It is quite conceivable that by a careful choice and arrangement of objects it might be possible to use the color on the projection surface artistically and harmoniously. But if the film image becomes stereoscopic there is no longer a plane surface within the confines of the screen, and therefore there can be no composition of that surface; what remains will be effects that are also possible on the stage. The increased size of the screen will render any two-dimensional or three-dimensional composition less compelling; and formative devices such as montage and changing camera angles will become unusable if the illusion of reality is so enormously strengthened. Obviously, montage will seem an intolerable accumulation of heterogeneous settings if the illusion of reality is very strong. Obviously also a change in the position of the camera will now be felt as an actual displacement within the space of the picture. The camera will have to become an immobile recording machine, every cut in the film strip will be mutilation. Scenes will have to be taken in their entire length and with a stationary camera, and they will have to be shown as they are. The artistic potentialities of this form of film will be exactly those of the stage. Film will no longer be able in any sense to be considered as a separate art. It will be thrown back to before its first beginnings—for it was with a fixed camera and an uncut strip that film started. The only difference will be that instead of having all before it film will have nothing to look forward to.

This curious development signifies to some extent the climax of that striving after likeness to nature which has hitherto permeated the whole history of the visual arts. Among the strivings that make human beings create faithful images is the primitive desire to get material objects into one's power by creating them afresh. Imitation also permits people to cope with significant experiences; it provides release, and makes for a kind of reciprocity between the self and the world. At the same time a reproduction that is true to nature provides the thrill that by the hand of man an image has been created which is astoundingly like some natural object. Nevertheless, various counter-tendencies—some of them purely perceptual—have prevented mechanically faithful imitation from being achieved hundreds of years ago. Apart from rare exceptions, only our modern age has succeeded in approaching this dangerous goal. In practice, there has always been the artistic urge not simply to copy but to originate, to interpret, to mold. We may, however, say that aesthetic theory has rarely sanctioned such activities. Even for artists like Leonardo da Vinci the demand for being as true to nature as possible was a matter of course when he talked theory, and Plato's attack on artists, in which he charged them with achieving nothing but reproductions of physical objects, is far from the general attitude.

To this very day some artists cherish this doctrine, and the general public does so to an even greater extent. In painting and sculpture it is only in recent decades that works have been appearing which show that their creators have broken with this principle intellectually and not merely practically. If a man considers that the artist should imitate nature, he may possibly paint like Van Gogh, but certainly not like Paul Klee. We know that the very powerful and widespread rejection of modern art is almost entirely supported by the argument that it is not true to nature. The development of film shows clearly how all-powerful this ideal still is.

Photography and its offspring, film, are art media so near to nature that the general public looks upon them as superior to such old-fashioned and imperfect imitative techniques as drawing and painting. Since on economic grounds film is much more dependent on the general public than any other form of art, the "artistic" preferences of the public sweep everything before them. Some work of good quality can be smuggled in but it does not compensate for the more fundamental defeats of film art. The complete film is the fulfillment of the age-old striving for the complete illusion. The attempt to make the two-dimensional picture as nearly as possible like its solid model succeeds; original and copy become practically indistinguishable. Thereby all formative potentialities which were based on the differences between model and copy are eliminated and only what is inherent in the original in the way of significant form remains to art.

H. Baer in a remarkable little essay in the *Kunstblatt* has pointed out that color film represents the accomplishment of tendencies which have long been present in graphic art.

"Graphic art (he says)—of which photography is one branch—has always striven after color. The oldest woodcuts, the blockbooks, were finished off by being handpainted. Later, a second, colored, plate was added to the black-and-white—as in Dürer's portrait of 'Ulrich Varnbühler.' A magnificent picture of a knight in armor in black, silver, and gold, exists by Burgmair. In the eighteenth century multicolored etchings were produced. In the nineteenth the lithographs of Daumier and Gavarni are colored in mass production . . . Color invaded the graphic arts as an increased attraction for the eye. Uncivilized man is not as a rule satisfied with black-and-white. Children, peasants and primitive peoples demand the highest degree of bright coloring. It is the primitives of the great cities who congregate before the film screen. Therefore film calls in the aid of bright colors. It is a fresh stimulus."

In itself, the perfection of the "complete" film need not be a catastrophe—if silent film, sound film, and colored sound film were allowed to exist alongside it. There is no objection to the "complete" film as an alternative to the stage—it might help to take into remote places fine performances of good works, as also of operas, musical comedies, ballets, the dance. Moreover, by its very existence it would probably have an excellent influence on the other—the real— film forms, by forcing them to advance along their own lines. Silent film, for example, would no longer provide dialogue in its titles, because then the absence of the spoken word would be felt as artificial and disturbing. In sound film, too, any vague intermediate form between it and the stage would be avoided. Just as the stage will feel itself obliged by the very existence of film to emphasize its own characteristic—the predominance of dramatic speech—so the "complete" film could relegate the true film forms to their own sphere.

The fact is, however, that whereas aesthetically these categories of film could and should exist along with mechanically complete reproduction, they are inferior to it in the capacity to imitate nature. Therefore the "complete" film is certain to be considered an advance upon the preceding film forms, and will supplant them all.

1933

THE THOUGHTS THAT
MADE THE PICTURE MOVE

Two basic technical properties characterize the film as we know it today: it reproduces the objects of our world photographically, that is, very faithfully, by means of a mechanical process on a two-dimensional surface; and it reproduces motion and events as accurately as it does the shape of things.

The ancient desire of man to make likenesses of his environment found new satisfaction when he became able to reproduce movement. Whatever the psychological causes of the wish to make likenesses may be, it will suffice here to point out that making images of events is even more important than depicting objects in their static shapes and colors because the fundamental biological reaction is that of reacting to happenings not that of contemplating objects. Correspondingly, the arts are greatly concerned from the beginning with things in action: hunting scenes, war, triumphal processions and funerals, dances and feasts.

Lively though such pictorial descriptions may look to us, they lack the distinguishing feature of events, namely, change in the course of time. Painting and sculpture are static arts: they can seize upon the

161

characteristic theme of an action and record it, but they cannot show its temporal unfolding.

Visual representation must either reproduce its subject with mechanical accuracy or—in the higher, aesthetic sense of the term—render its essentials faithfully. In addition, representation must fixate the image so that it may be preserved and looked at again at any time. When actors perform a play or when primitive dancers portray the hunter and his game, they create representations that lack the essential property of fixation. From the beginning, man has excelled in making durable but immobile pictures. Up to our own day, he has hardly succeeded in presenting motion by motion in such a way as to obtain a faithful and readily available reproduction. Even film does not meet this specification: it does not render motion by motion but gives an illusion of it by means of immobile images shown in sequence—a procedure that is possible because of the way our eyes work, a magnificent substitute, but something fundamentally different from the rendering of motion by motion.

Why, then, did we have to resort to illusory movement? Why has the theoretically most obvious solution hardly been employed at all? There is no obstacle in principle—the reasons are mainly technical. Man is capable of making his body carry out movement and he also has put at his service mechanisms that will execute required actions as often as desired and in practically identical fashion. The machines used for manufacture perform the most intricate motions. But little useful machinery has been developed for the mechanical imitation of natural events. Marionettes and shadow figures do render action, but basically they resemble the theater in that they are not controlled mechanically but by the human hand. Granted, there are robots guided by clockworks or electricity. There are wooden figures doffing their hats or pointing at the merchandise in shop windows. Museums exhibit animated models of factories and mines, in which hundreds of small workers and machines are shown in busy action. All such devices fulfill the condition of fixating motion mechanically and of making it reproducible at any time without need of human steering; but nothing better than toys has been made so far, nothing that could be used artistically—various monsters of the horror movies notwithstanding.

In short, the representations of motion are either controlled by human action, in which case they do not record mechanically, or they are mechanical, but too primitive. In theory, it would be conceivable to produce a satisfactory animated reproduction in two or three dimensions, which showed human figures in natural action, leaves moved by the wind, water purling over rocks, clouds drifting across the sky— all this in actual motion, steered by machinery. Perhaps such an animated scene could be produced on a surface by means of iron filings controlled from the back by mechanically steered magnets.

Theater machinists have no trouble in making clouds move by projecting them on the backdrop. The motion required here is simple and straight, and quite generally the actions reproduced nowadays by such devices are either simple and straight in themselves or are controlled by such uncomplicated motions.

Photography has raised our demands: we like reproductions not only to be faithful to the object but also to guarantee their faithfulness by being mechanical manifestations of the reproduced object itself. The objects that are photographed impinge their own images mechanically upon the sensitive emulsion. Are there reproductions of movement that satisfy this condition?

There is indeed the remarkable instance of a physical process that fixates its own motion mechanically in such a way that when the tracing is used later for reproduction, a most faithful performance results, which renders all the natural detail of the original. Significantly enough, this example does not come from the realm of visible things: it is the process of sound recording. All music, voices, and other noises, complex though they may be psychologically, can be reduced physically to a vibratory movement, which does justice to all auditory qualities by means of the amplitude, frequency, and shape of the vibrations. Sound-recording devices make the sound vibrations impress their own path, either mechanically upon wax, shellac, or plastic, or photoelectrically upon film by a beam of light. In the reproduction the tracks that have been obtained in this manner act like rails and thus help produce a movement that is practically identical with the original one. We notice, however, that although the sounds rendered by these techniques are quite complex, the visual shapes used in the process are nothing but one-dimensional lines or very simple otherwise.

Among the predecessors of cinematography there are some contraptions that made movement reproduce movement, although in a primitive fashion. This was done either by moving the pictures themselves or by moving their projected image optically, or, finally, by projecting upon a mobile medium. The Laterna Magica that was constructed in the seventeenth century by the mathematician Milliet de Chales used glass slides introduced from the side. This technique not only suggested putting a sequence of several pictures on the same slide and showing them in succession but also having one scene glide through the visual field in a continuous motion, thus imitating the impression one gets when looking through the window of a car. The same principle operated in the so-called *Vues Optiques,* with which the Savoyard boys traveled. Through an enlarging eyepiece the public watched painted or printed scenes, which were commonly wound on reels and pulled through the box laterally by means of a crank. It is worth noticing that the movement reproduced here by real movement is an illusory one, namely, the subjective experience of seeing the world slide by the window. In physical reality, such a primitively simple displacement of the entire setting does not occur.

The displacement of the entire picture, crude though it is, helps considerably to animate the performance, particularly since the mechanism that produces the motion is hidden from sight. A useful demonstration of how much the choice of subject matter and the way of presenting it depend on the nature of the recording instrument is evidenced in that later, when the actual motion-picture camera was in use, traveling shots of landscapes were not at all obvious but had to be invented all over again, as it were, although the practically identical effect had been known for centuries. Mr. M. A. Promio who toured Europe in 1896 with the new Lumière apparatus, as a camera reporter and projectionist combined in one person, writes: "In Italy, it occurred to me for the first time to make traveling shots. After arriving in Venice I took the boat from the station to my hotel. When I saw the buildings along the Canale Grande move by, I had the idea that the film camera, which could take pictures of moving things while it was standing still, perhaps could take immobile things while it was moving itself. I took a sample film and sent it to Mr. Louis Lumière, asking him for his opinion. The reaction was positive." Mr. Promio's idea has all the virtues of a genuine invention even though what he found was not new historically. The old effect, namely, the moving landscape, is arrived at from an entirely new starting point, and in the process the principle of relativity, on which the effect is based, is formulated explicitly: in motion pictures, movement is not absolute but always related to the station point of the camera. Here, then, a pioneer considered the properties of the recording technique in a way that later on led to the development of film as art. To conceive of the idea that the camera was not simply a passive receiver of what was moving around in front of the lens, but could take an active part, for instance, by moving itself, was a first step in the direction of progress. It was much less obvious to make the camera move than to move pictures through the peep-show box.

In the *Vues Optiques* the image moved as a whole. Therefore, it was not possible with this technique to make a human figure move in front of an immobile background. But by leaving out all background one could present a moving figure without giving away the fact that actually the whole field was moving. Some such device may also have played a part in certain conjuring shows, in which projected figures were made to appear getting larger or smaller by moving the Laterna Magica backward or forward. There are reports from antiquity to suggest that even then such tricks were known, including the use of lenses and concave mirrors. Damasius, as cited by Coissac, describes how a "mass of light" appeared on the wall of a temple in Alexandria. At first, it seemed to be very far away, and as it approached it changed into what was taken to be the supernatural apparition of a figure. Probably this exciting effect was produced by beginning the projection out of focus and gradually moving the lens until the picture of the figure could be seen sharply. A more elaborate system was used by the magician E. G. Robertson, who at the time of the French Revolution made the effigies of the dead appear to a puzzled audience. He compensated the movement of the lantern by changing the position of the lens and thereby was able to show a figure growing larger and remaining in sharp focus throughout the change. In this manner he obtained the compelling impression of an approaching figure— an effect that is brought about more comfortably nowadays by lenses of variable magnification (so-called zoom lenses). It is not unlikely that sometimes Robertson projected on smoke, which produced distorted, moving images. This trick, too, seems to have a long history—compare, for instance, Benvenuto Cellini's description of the apparition of ghosts in the Colosseum.

What all these procedures have in common is that

the movement is not derived from the reproduced objects themselves but is imposed upon the picture from the outside. The effects thus attainable, namely, lateral displacement, or change of total size, or irregular distortion will not produce characteristic likeness unless by accident or in a rather primitive fashion.

Since attempts to represent movement by movement had not been very successful, illusory movement attracted the attention of inventors. They found that they could create the impression of movement by combining still pictures with each other. A curious theoretical question arises here: is there not an inherent contradiction in trying to fixate changing things? How can we record a given phase of a movement at the same place at which a moment before we recorded the preceding phase, permanently—since it is permanent recording we are after?

At this point it is necessary to introduce a distinction between two different tasks accomplished by film: it presents a picture of motion, such as that of a runner, or a dancer, or a mower, and it also renders the successive phases of events. In principle there is no sharp division between the two functions since they both derive from the capacity to record changes that occur within the dimension of time. Yet in practice the difference is evident and quite important, so much so that in the visual arts the two kinds of activity are represented in totally different ways.

Momentary motion has always been represented in the arts by showing the limbs of the human body in active positions: running legs, fighting arms, gestures of grief, dance positions. The course of an action in time, on the other hand, could never be presented by a single image—it always had to be a series. It suffices to think of the stations of the cross, or the stories of the lives of the saints. Temporal sequence is translated into spatial sequence, the continuum of the story is divided up into phases, and the same figure returns in several representations, be it in several pictures or within the frame of one, thus splitting its identity.

This distribution of successive phases over a series of pictures and the related splitting of identity—that is, the technique used in painting and sculpture only for the purpose of representing the stages of a story—turned out to be the best way for the film to portray live, momentary motion. There was a profound difference, of course: in film, the single pictures of the sequence exist only technically, not in what is experienced by the audience. As far as the eyes of the spectators go, there is no synthesis of phases but an indivisible continuum. The principle of synthesis reappears in the movies only when scenes that were taken separately are spliced together in montage in such a way that discontinuities of time and space are suggested.

It sounds paradoxical, I said before, to want to fixate the mobile by means of the immobile. Which solutions of this problem are there available in principle?

1) If we make a photographic time exposure of a person who is standing in front of the camera and, without moving from his place, changes the expression of his face, the result will be a blurred picture because the successive phases of the facial expression will have been recorded one on top of the other. That is, one

cannot simply ignore the time dimension—some equivalent has to be found for it. The recording of periodic events represents a borderline case: the photograph of an oscillating pendulum, for instance, will produce at least sharp images of the extreme positions on each side. This opportunity was used in 1865 by Onimus and Martin, who photographed the movement of the living heart in vivisectional experiments. (These attempts represent the beginnings of the so-called chronophotography, whose main pioneer was the physiologist Etienne Jules Marey.) Since the motion of the heart comes to a kind of standstill and turns direction at the moments of the greatest expansion and contraction, the two limiting phases were clearly recorded on the photographic plate. Notice that the procedure is applicable only when, strictly speaking, motion has come to a standstill, and also when the phases to be recorded happen to fall upon different places on the photographic plate. The special character of periodic movement is made particularly evident by the fact that it can give the impression of complete rest. This happens when of each period of movement only one, and always the same, momentary phase is singled out for observation. In order to control the regularity of the rotation in machines, the stroboscope is used. If the apertures of the stroboscope are exposed exactly at the rate of the rotation, the same phase of the motion is seen every time, and the machine seems to stand still. Here, then, a succession of exposures at the same place produces a sharp and clear image because the phases thus superimposed upon one another are identical.

2) When the object to be photographed changes its

location on the plate while it is moving, the phases that follow each other in time can be presented next to each other in space. If, for example, the object moves across the field, the path of the movement will be faithfully recorded. The finest illustration of this principle is a time exposure of the starry sky. Every star appears as a bright circular line. The procedure is applicable because the objects to be photographed are nothing but light dots and the background is plain black. There are no shapes to get blurred by their displacement on the plate.

According to Marey, however, chronophotography has two tasks: it must record the path of the movement and also the positions of the object in various stages. The second task obviously cannot be solved with the present procedure since the various phases overlap in such a way that their images cancel each other out.

3) The next requirement, then, is that of breaking up the continuum into separate sharp images. The recording of the movement has to be interrupted periodically, and the resulting exposures must be short enough to yield sharp pictures. Naturally, this presupposes a sufficiently sensitive photographic emulsion or a sufficiently strong light source. The modern high-speed methods have reduced the exposure time to less than one ten-thousandth of a second. Daguerre had to leave his lens open for several minutes in order to take a picture, but even Eadweard Muybridge in the 1870's took snapshots at one six-thousandth of a second, and the emulsions he used would have permitted him to use even shorter exposures if his cameras had permitted him to do so.

Obviously, the faster the object moves, the shorter the exposure time has to be in order to give sharp pictures. Also, the faster the movement, the shorter the time interval between subsequent pictures must be (other factors being equal) if all essential phases of the action are to be recorded. For example, Marey's "photographic rifle," which took twelve pictures per second was not fast enough to record the phases of the flight of birds.

By what means was the exposure interrupted? Daguerre could take the lid off the lens and hold it in his hand until time was up. Ottomar Anschütz used for his serial photographs the kind of shutter that is found in every photocamera today and that had been invented by Jules Janssen in 1874. This mechanism, however, is impractical when the camera is expected to take several pictures in quick succession. For this reason, Janssen constructed a rotating shutter disk, which made it possible for his "photographic pistol" to take forty-eight pictures in a row. The rotating disk was perforated by slots, which let the light pass and thereby exposed the emulsion briefly at the desired intervals. A similar effect can be obtained by interrupting the light source periodically. This is one of the methods used in scientific high-speed photography today; but already in 1887 Anschütz mounted series of slides on the rotating disk of his "electrotachyscope" and lighted them for the purpose of projection by intermittently flashing vacuum tubes.

The periodic interruption of the exposure definitely reduces the recording of movement to the taking of static pictures. If the exposure time is short enough, the motion of the object approaches zero, and the picture will be sharp. The action to be recorded is now composed of separate phases; nevertheless, it is more fitting historically to speak of analysis rather than of synthesis because the originally unitary movement has been decomposed into partial images.

In Marey's chronophotography the fixation of sequences on the immobile negative was used for purely scientific research in physiology. Motion was to be analyzed, not reproduced in projection. Even so, chronophotography represents an important preparatory stage in the development toward the motion picture, which involves the decomposition of the action as a first step.

Marey's technique could be applied only to objects that moved parallel to the picture plane—a condition he was able to fulfill in his experiments. Also since he opened the entire negative to the light every time, he had to see to it that it was not spoiled by premature exposure. Suppose a person running in front of a landscape were photographed in this fashion; every time the negative would be exposed in order to record a new phase of the running, the entire landscape would also register, that is, the plate would no longer be sensitive to the picture of the man. Marey was compelled, therefore, to take his pictures against a black background—another considerable limitation, as far as any more general use of the technique was concerned. And finally, of course, the movement had to take place within the immobile range of the camera. If the recorded movement was to cover a reasonably large span, it had to be photographed from a fairly great distance—which means that the pictures thus obtained were necessarily small. Also, the orientation of the object toward the camera changed during the displacement, that is, the perspective appearance of the object did not remain constant.

4) One step further, and a different piece of negative is reserved for each picture. The plate is still immobile so that there are only two possible solutions: either the lens moves in front of the plate, or a whole sequence of cameras is used to take one picture each. No historical example of the first procedure seems to be known; the second is used in the serial photographs of Muybridge (1877) and Anschütz (1885).

When a group of cameras photograph the moving object in succession, a set of phases is recorded. But since several cameras cannot be set up in the same place, the station point keeps changing. If they are arranged in a row, the result will look in the projection like a traveling shot—an effect that is welcome occasionally, for instance, when the object moves along the row of cameras. Under other conditions, the resulting parallax might produce a vexing problem, however, as shown, for instance, by the apparatus of Augustin le Prince. He mounted a number of lenses in two circular arrangements, which alternately photographed the objects on two different strips of film. When Joseph Mason undertook to demonstrate the efficiency of this arrangement experimentally by projecting the pictures, he had to take figures on a black background, cut the film strip into single pictures, and correct the displacements in such a way that the figures taken from two different visual angles appeared nevertheless in the same spot of the visual field. Parallactic displacement is particularly disturbing when several pictures that are taken at the same time of the same object, must be combined as is done in certain color film systems. This produces a spatial parallax, whereas a temporal parallax—equally undesirable—results when the pictures of the moving object are taken from the same place, but one after the other. Stereoscopic film, on the other hand, makes use of the parallax by combining in the mind of the observer two pictures taken from slightly different viewpoints; it thus obtains the same kind of three-dimensional effect as do a person's two eyes.

In the serial photographs of Muybridge and Anschütz, then, the relationship between camera and moving object was kept constant by using a different camera for recording each phase along the path. Race horses, goats, or ostriches released with their running feet each camera at the exact moment when they passed through the field of its lens. By this method the releasing mechanism was made dependent on the movement of the object. In consequence, the pictures were taken at constant intervals only when the object happened to move at constant speed. But at least it was possible now to record a series of phases on a series of negatives, which were exposed individually. The mutual independence of the single pictures had been accomplished definitely and thoroughly.

5) None of the methods so far described was "film" as we know it today. The history of human ingenuity shows that almost every innovation goes through a preliminary phase in which the solution is obtained by the old method, modified or amplified by some new feature. Just as the first motorcars looked like horse-drawn carriages but had motors built in, so the first photographic recordings of motion were based on the

traditional still camera: they were done either with one camera on one negative or by a combination of several cameras.

The decisive invention consisted in making available a new piece of negative for each new phase of the moving object. Up to that point the negative had remained immobile, and therefore it had been up to the object to coöperate by moving in such a way that each phase photographed on a different area of the plate. As soon as the negative is made to move, the object may remain in one and the same place, and a series of pictures may still be taken from the same spot.

In some of the early apparatuses several pieces of negative were mounted on a mobile carrier. Marey's photographic rifle contained a small rotating glass disk on the margin of which twelve pieces of negative were mounted. In others, one large negative was exposed a sufficient number of times while it rotated in the camera. Thus in Janssen's photographic pistol, by means of which the inventor photographed the phases of the transit of the planet Venus in front of the sun on December 9, 1874, forty-eight pictures were made on the margin of the negative. The method of using one negative is somewhat more convenient as far as developing and printing are concerned, and therefore it has prevailed. Today's film technique uses one negative, the film strip, which is exposed portion by portion.

In the first cameras the pictures were arranged in circles. Presumably this was the most efficient method available for inflexible negative plates. The discovery of celluloid is historically later than the first attempts to photograph motion by means of mobile negatives; hence the rotating negative plates.

A combination of rotation and linear displacement is attributed to Edison. He is said to have arranged negatives in a spiral on a cylinder—an idea obviously influenced by the principle of his phonograph cylinders. The spiral uses space more economically than the circle on the disk, but the flexible celluloid base won out over both. The use of a spiral arrangement on a disk by W. Friese-Greene in 1885 should be mentioned, nevertheless, as well as an experiment in which rows of six pictures each were photographed in a zigzag scanning motion on one plate. This latter principle, remindful of the modern television technique, has found no further application in the motion-picture field so far, although the cameraman Guido Seeber has pointed out that it might regain interest if microscopically small negatives could be made. Some other principles, known from the history of the projection technique, seem never to have been tried for the taking of pictures: there is the arrangement on the outside of a drum or on the spokes of a paddle wheel or the booklet type used in Linnett's kineograph of 1868 or Casler's mutoscope of 1894.

With the adoption of the flexible base, the last resemblance to the old photographic glass plate became a thing of the past. The first material to be used was not celluloid. Friese-Greene tried oiled paper, and Eastman also experimented with paper before the first paperless film was put on the market as roll film in 1889. Among the first customers were the Edison Photographic Works in Orange.

The movement of the base is not sufficient to solve

the fundamental problem since a blurred picture results when the object is recorded on a continuously moving plate or film. The motion of the object itself is an additional source of blur. The theoretically simplest solution is that of making the exposure time for each image so short that the movement of the negative as well as that of the object will be reduced practically to zero. But with so short an exposure time even the strongest light will produce fairly dark pictures. Therefore this technique has been used only for the kind of slow-motion shots that require 250 pictures or more per second and for which the normal modern procedure of intermittent movement would be too hard on the camera and the film. The scientific purposes of such high-speed photography are often satisfied by shadow-like outline pictures of the moving object.

When, however, normal, well-lighted pictures are desired, the negative material of the kind that is available today requires longer exposures. A rather intricate solution is offered by what is known as optical compensation. The movement of the negative carrier remains continuous, but an optical system of rotating glass slabs makes the image of the lens accompany the moving negative long enough to increase the exposure time somewhat. This means that an additional movement is introduced for the purpose of compensating the relative displacement of negative versus lens. This principle also is used only for high-speed work.

The method commonly applied nowadays abandons the continuous motion of the base: the negative is arrested during each exposure. This means that the motion picture, after having emancipated itself from still photography by introducing the principle of the mobile base, returns to snapshot photography, although at a higher technical level: the photograph is made again on an immobile negative, but after each exposure the negative is replaced by means of an efficient mechanism. The translation of the continuous movement into intermittent movement is achieved either by a so-called claw, which engages the sprocket holes of the film and pulls the negative down, frame by frame, or by a Maltese cross, which moves the film by intermittent rotation. A shutter serves to withhold the light while the negative moves. The Maltese cross was used already around the middle of the nineteenth century by Molteni, who projected animated cartoons from an intermittently rotating disk. Janssen used the same device for his photographic pistol, whereas a claw mechanism served—for shooting, printing, and projecting alike—in Lumière's famous *Cinématographe*. Nowadays the Maltese cross is used mostly in projectors, the claw for cameras.

Finally, a word should be said about the source of energy that produces the motion. Janssen and Marey moved their rotating disks by clockworks, which are forerunners of our modern electric and spring motors. The early film cameras were, of course, operated by crank, but even then the activating movement was continuous. Only in animation work each frame is exposed by a separate move. This technical feature may help to illustrate the fact that the motion picture is not a synthetic agglomeration of individual images but based on a recording process that is as continuous and unitary as the movement of the photographed objects. The dividing of the movement into single "frames" (just as their subsequent unification in the projection) is nothing but a technical detail, which does not concern the nature of the procedure. There is, then, a difference in principle between the recording of visual motion and the immobile images of photography, painting, or sculpture. Film is more than a variation of the immobile image, obtained by multiplication: it is fundamentally new and different.

1934

MOTION

The motion picture specializes in presenting events. It shows changes in time. This preference is explained by the nature of the medium. A motion picture in itself is an event: it looks different every moment, whereas there is no such temporal progress in a painting or sculpture. Motion being one of its outstanding properties, the film is required by aesthetic law to use and interpret motion.

The technically most characteristic motion of the cinematographic process, however, must not be counted among the means of expression of which the motion picture profits: the displacement of the film strip in the camera and in the projector is not experienced directly by the audience. It is simply the mechanical means of creating the illusion of motion on the screen; also, the speed of the film strip in the camera as compared with the speed of projection indirectly determines the speed of the movements seen by the spectator. But the beat of the intermittent motion in the camera and the projector has no bearing upon the aesthetic rhythm of the picture.

Motion as it is actually experienced by the audience relies on the following factors: (1) the movements of the objects, alive or dead, that are photographed by the camera; (2) the effect of perspective and of the distance of the camera from the object; (3) the effect of the moving camera; (4) the synthesis of individual scenes, accomplished by montage, in an over-all composition of motion; (5) the interaction of movements that are put next to each other by montage.

Motion not only serves to inform the audience of the events that make up the story. It is also highly expressive. When we watch a mother putting her child to bed we not only understand what is going on but also learn from the calm or hasty, smooth or fumbling, energetic or weak, sure or hesitant gestures of the mother what kind of person she is, how she feels at the particular moment, and what her relationship is to her child. The contrast between the irrational struggling of the infant and the controlled behavior of the mother may produce a counterpoint of visual motion, which determines the expression of the scene at least as effectively as do the more static factors of how mother and child look and in what kind of setting the action takes place.

It is the task of the actors and the director to emphasize the expressive qualities of motion and thereby to define the character of the entire film as well as that of the single scene and the single shot. In the same manner the various personalities in their similarities and differences will be defined visually. Even on the stage, motion is thus exploited artistically; but this is all the more true for film, where things appear closer and sharper and where the direction and speed of each motion is set off clearly by the narrow rectangular frame of the image. If a given character or a given scene can be embodied in a musically articulate, impressive theme of movement, the gain for the picture will be twofold: the content will be interpreted to the eye, and the appearance of the moving objects will acquire artistic shape.

On the stage as well as in film, the great actor is distinguished by a simple, characteristic melody of movement all his own. This is most easily seen in extreme cases, such as those of Chaplin or Keaton, where the particular dynamic theme can be defined with the precision of musical terms. (Compare here, for instance, the acting of their fellow comedian Harold Lloyd, who, not being a great artist, has no such personal melody of movement.) The common narrative film cannot stress the form qualities of gesture and gait to the same extent since this would not be in keeping with a realistic style of performance; but even there a good actor will clearly distinguish, by his motion, strength from weakness, straightforwardness from guile, beauty from ugliness. When in *Grand Hotel* Greta Garbo walked through the lobby with a springy, dynamic gait, she produced not only the most beautiful moment of the film but also perhaps the most telling characterization of the dancer, whose part she was playing. At the risk of doing an injustice to the most animated face in the history of film art, it may be said that Greta Garbo could give equally strong expression to the human soul by the rhythm of her gait, which, depending upon the occasion, was victorious and energetic, transfigured, or tired, broken, anxious, and feeble.

The films of the early years were less realistic and therefore expressed the various dramatic types by motions of graphic simplicity. There was musical purity and beauty in the graceful leaps of Douglas Fairbanks and the heavy stamping of Paul Wegener's Golem. Unquestionably the greater "lifelikeness" of the later style has robbed the film play of much of its melodic shape. There was, in those early pantomimes, a dance-like quality, which was most filmic and should not remain lost forever.

Motion is not limited to the actor. In film, man is always an inextricable part of his environment. The environment shares in the acting and produces motion that can be more impressive than that of the human body. The stubborn resistance of a strong man to a storm is effectively underscored when at the same time trees are seen to bend, and the inexorable rotations of the windmill, which not only cannot be interrupted by Don Quixote but defeat him by carrying him off, symbolize the rigid course of the world, against which human rebellion is powerless. In *Shanghai Express,* the teeming crowds in a Chinese railway station serve as a contrasting foil to the quiet intensity of a love scene. The drifting of clouds, the waves of the wind over a wheat field, the onrush of a waterfall, the swing of a pendulum, the up and down of pistons have lent more impact to many a film scene than all the gestures of the actors. This is not surprising for the actions of the inorganic world have a grandiose simplicity, which is not easily matched by the complex instrument of the human mind.

The expressive quality of any movement is dependent on its speed, and by changing the speed of natural movements film can modify their character. Within narrow limits the cameramen of the old school, who operated their cameras by turning the crank, would subtly correct movements by slowing them down or speeding them up according to the wishes of the director. A hasty gesture could be made smoother, a fast action more clearly visible; and on the other hand, vigor could be added to a sluggish thrust. This flexibility of the camera speed was lost when the sound film standardized the number of frames to be exposed per second; and ever since, this opportunity of correcting the shape of motion has been neglected. More fundamental changes are, of course, accomplished through the special devices for slow motion and acceleration.

Movement that looks natural in reality tends to be too fast on the screen—presumably because film shows most of the action from relatively close quarters. The nearer we are to the motion, the larger is the area of our visual field that it crosses and the faster it appears correspondingly. The experienced actor in the studio seems unnaturally slow, and close-ups in particular must be acted at reduced speed. This psychological requirement was not acknowledged in the early days: things happened with theatrical velocity, and the haste of the gestures tends to look ludicrous now. The effect of distance upon the speed of perceived motion can also be studied from the front rows of the motion-picture theater: when the screen covers a large area of the visual field, movements extend over relatively long distances and therefore look fast.

Rhythm is closely related to motion. Repetition, for example, exerts its spell in the movies as it does in nature, witness the visual intensity of scenes showing marching soldiers, men at work, engines, or kicking choruses. But it is not sufficient to discuss only the motions of objects in themselves. The way these motions appear on the screen is considerably influenced by the technique of recording and combining them. The particular angle at which the camera captures the object will influence movement, not only because speed depends upon distance but also because perspective foreshortening will diminish the path of the movement, that is, increase visual speed. Oblique shots, therefore, will often intensify movement, thus adding the dynamics of velocity to that of slanted position.

Furthermore, any displacement of the camera produces and modifies movement. Traveling shots show objects in illusory movement, even though reason tries to remind us that they actually are immobile. Objects that are at different distances from the camera appear displaced with regard to each other when their picture is taken, for instance, from a moving train; and objects will appear to go faster, more slowly, or stand still, depending on the direction and speed of the moving camera.

After a scene has been taken, the motions it records undergo further modifications in the cutting room. A section of a movement, cut from its original context, is likely to change its quality, and the combination of movements in montage causes a good deal of mutual interference. Movements that oppose and thus balance each other are often shown together: in the first scene a train travels from the left to the right, in the second a door closes from the right to the left. Or the parallel directions of two movements are used to suggest a comparison between the two scenes. Again, an action seems slowed down when it is flanked by faster ones; and vice versa. Excessive contrast may break the continuity. Good editing will provide enough variety of speed, direction, and location of movement, but at the same time preserve the necessary unity. Any sequence should have a clearly defined pattern of movement, be it that the increasing speed of the scenes that follow each other builds up a crescendo, or that the controlled succession of fast and slow units creates a definite rhythm.

Montage influences speed in that motion looks the faster, the shorter the time of its exposure. When short pieces follow each other in rapid succession, intense dynamics result, which may suit a dramatic episode but may have to be smoothed by dissolves otherwise.

Since visual movement is action that takes place in the course of time it has an affinity with music and is influenced by it. Music can underscore the dynamic character of movement on the screen most effectively, as shown, for instance, in the whistles, signs, and thuds of the animated cartoon. Music also tends to give wings to motion and therefore may help to recapture some of the dancelike stylization that got lost when the pictures began to emulate nature too closely.

1935

A FORECAST OF
TELEVISION

Man's range of interest goes beyond the reach of his senses. Of the technical inventions that serve to diminish this disproportion, television is the latest and perhaps the most important. The new gadget seems magical and mysterious. It arouses curiosity: How does it work? What does it do to us? To be sure, when the television sets will have appeared on the birthday tables and under the Christmas trees, curiosity will abate. Mystery asks for explanation only as long as it is new. Let us take advantage of the propitious moment.

First of all, what is the fundamental problem involved in television? Eyes and ears have quite different tasks and, correspondingly, are made differently. The eye gives information about shape, color, surface qualities, and motion of objects in three-dimensional space by registering the reactions of these objects to light. The ear reveals little about the objects as such; it only reports on some of their activities, which happen to produce sound waves. On the whole, the eye takes little interest in the nature, place, and condition of the light sources that make the light rays fall upon the retina. The ear is interested in the source of the sound; it wants the sound waves, on their way to the eardrum, to be as little modified as possible in order to keep the message from the source unaltered. Sound is produced by an object but tells us little about that object's shape, whereas the eye, in order to fulfill its task, must reckon with the fact that a suitable likeness of a three-dimensional object must be at least two-dimensional. The projection of a three-dimensional body upon a two-dimensional plane will give a one-sided but often informative picture. No satisfactory information would be obtained after the even more radical reduction of a body to a one-dimensional object—whether the reduction be spatial, that is, like a line on paper, or temporal, that is, a sequence of changes taking place in one point.

Any sense organ can register only one stimulus at a time so that the eye in order to produce a two-dimensional recording has to consist of numerous receptors that operate one next to the other. The mosaic that results from this collaboration of the receptors depicts three-dimensional space and volume as best it can. The time dimension, which is available in addition, uses the change of stimulation in each receptor to record motion and action.

A different situation is found in hearing. The sounds that exist in auditory space at any one time are not recorded separately but add up to one, more or less complex vibration, which can be received by a single membrane, such as the eardrum. This unitary vibration may be produced by the simple sound of a tuning fork or the complex noises of a crowd of excited people or a symphony orchestra. To some extent the ear succeeds in teasing the complex vibration apart, but it offers scant information about the locations of the different sound sources. The ear, like the eye, operates with a battery of receptors, and they, too, are arranged in a two-dimensional surface. The receptors of the cochlea are parallel fibers, as different in length and tension as the strings of a harp, and apparently for a similar purpose. The "strings" of the cochlea seem to be activated by resonance when vibrations of corresponding frequencies impinge upon them. This means that the ear uses its receptor field to distinguish between pitches, whereas the eye uses its to distinguish between spatial locations.

Whatever our hearing tells us about space and the directions from which sounds reach us is not strictly indispensable. Radio and phonograph often eliminate the resonance that gives information about space, and never tell about the direction but only about the distance of the sound source from the microphone. Auditory space, as transmitted by these mechanical devices, knows neither right nor left, neither above nor below. It only distinguishes between near and far, and yet we receive a rather complete or at least satisfactory impression. Whatever spatial qualities *are* transmitted, are derived from modifications sustained by the sound as it moves through space: distant sound is blurred, it is relatively weaker, and so forth.

If we do without directional hearing, the ear needs only three kinds of data, namely, the amplitude of the vibration, which produces loudness, the speed of the vibration, which produces pitch, and the shape of the vibration, which produces timbre (the difference between a flute, a bell, a soprano, a dog's bark). Since all the sounds that occur at a given moment fuse into one complex vibration, only one receptor is needed for the physical recording and transportation of sound. The eye, on the other hand, has to deal with millions of point-sized stimuli, which constitute the visual field. Therefore, in order to see space, volume, and shape, we require a battery of innumerable eyes—all of which are served by one common lens in the human receptor organ whereas insects have individual lenses for every eye. The sensitive surface formed by these eyes reproduces a projection of three-dimensional space.

These are the conditions that determine our modern ways of sending pictures, music, and speech through space. When light and sound do the transmitting themselves, the result is not very accurate even though the distance may be relatively small and our eyes and ears reinforced by mechanical receptor devices. Colors fade, shapes become fuzzy, sounds are blurred as the vibrations that carry them travel through space. In vision, the size of the retinal image depends on the visual angle, which may make objects shrink beyond recognition even at moderate distances. Therefore, definite progress was made as soon as it became possible to translate properties of sound and light messages into properties of electrical waves, for these waves travel through open space or wire without undergoing relevant changes; they adapt themselves to the curvature of the earth, and their speed is so nearly infinite that emission and reception become practically simultaneous. Space and time are annihilated.

It still strikes us as uncanny that pictures can be sent by telephone, and that we can see by radio. This is so because the electric transmission of sound was invented first. There is nothing inherently more or less mysterious in the one than in the other. The electrical waves will transmit the equivalents of amplitude, frequency, and shape of vibration, that is, all the essential properties of the phenomena in question. The particular problem of television is, of course, that pictures are two-dimensional. If analyzed, they decompose into a large number of brightness and color values, only one of which can be transmitted by one transmitter at a given moment. If we consider that the retina of the eye employs something like one hundred and fifty million receptors to produce an image, it seems that millions of telephones or radio stations should be needed to send just one picture. Fortunately, our eyes retain a given impression for a definite, though small span of time so that if all the stimuli that make up the picture are shown within a fraction of a second they will seem to appear all at once. Short though these time intervals need to be, they are long enough for electricity to send the point-sized stimuli one after the other over one and the same transmitter. The problem has been solved, in other words, by translating spatial relations (within the picture) into temporal ones, that is, by transforming a two-dimensional phenomenon into a one-dimensional one.

Speed of transmission is necessary also because visual objects change and move. The motion picture has taught us that a minimum of sixteen to twenty-four images per second is needed to produce smooth motion. Therefore the cathode ray must scan any one image fast enough to deal with a sufficient number of them every second. The scanning device must take care of the first, the second, and the fourth dimensions practically all at once.

Television enormously increases the capacity of radio for documentary information. The auditory world, available to the listener, is poor in documentary qualities. Hearing excels in transmitting speech and music, that is, products of the spirit; it renders little of physical reality. Without the services of a commentator or reporter, the event that radio purports to send over the air waves remains fragmentary to the point of being incomprehensible. Sometimes the rhythmical noise of marching feet, the scraps of band music and voices may add up to the picture of a large crowd moving through the streets of a city. But the concreteness of such an experience is more to the credit of the listener's imagination than to what comes actually through the loud-speaker. The ear is a tool of reasoning; it is best qualified to receive material that has been given shape by man already—whereas seeing is direct experience, the gathering of sensory raw material.

Through television radio becomes a documentary medium. Only when it ministers also to the eye, radio fulfills its task—not its only task and perhaps not its most important—of making us witness immediately what is going on in the wide world around us. We see the citizens of a neighboring town assembled in the market square, the Prime Minister of a foreign country making a speech, two boxers fighting for the world championship in an arena across the ocean, the British dance bands performing, an Italian coloratura singer, a German professor, the smoldering remains of a wrecked railway train, the masked street crowds at the carnival, the snow-capped mountains of the Alps as they appear through clouds from an airplane, tropical fish through the windows of a submarine, the machines of a car factory, an explorer's ship battling the polar ice. We see the sun shining on Mount Vesuvius and, a second later, the neon lights that illuminate Broadway at the same time. The detour via the describing word becomes unnecessary, the barrier of foreign languages loses importance. The wide world itself enters our room.

Television is a relative of motorcar and airplane: it is a means of cultural transportation. To be sure, it is a mere instrument of transmission, which does not offer new means for the artistic interpretation of reality—as radio and film did. But like the transportation machines, which were a gift of the last century, television changes our attitude to reality: it makes us know the world better and in particular gives us a feeling for the multiplicity of what happens simultaneously in different places. For the first time in the history of man's striving for understanding, simultaneity can be experienced as such, not merely as translated into a succession in time. Our slow bodies and nearsighted eyes no longer hamper us. We come to recognize the place where we are located as one among many: we become more modest, less egocentric.

The technical gadget of the television set, however, does not cause these beneficial changes by itself. It offers possibilities, which the public must seize. Although the new victory over time and space represents an impressive enrichment of the perceptual world, it also favors the cult of sensory stimulation, which is characteristic of the cultural attitude of our time. Proud of our inventions—photography, the phonograph, film, radio—we praise the educational virtues of direct experience. We believe in traveling, and use pictures and movies in the schools. But as we render man's image of his world immensely more complete and accurate than it was in the past, we also restrict the realm of the spoken and the written word and thereby the realm of thinking. The more perfect our means of direct experience, the more easily we are caught by the dangerous illusion that perceiving is tantamount to knowing and understanding.

Television is a new, hard test of our wisdom. If we succeed in mastering the new medium it will enrich us. But it can also put our mind to sleep. We must not forget that in the past the inability to transport immediate experience and to convey it to others made the use of language necessary and thus compelled the human mind to develop concepts. For in order to describe things one must draw the general from the specific; one must select, compare, think. When communication can be achieved by pointing with the finger, however, the mouth grows silent, the writing hand stops, and the mind shrinks.

A good documentary or educational film is not raw experience. The material has passed the mill of reason, it has been sifted and interpreted. The direct transmissions of television will not offer much opportunity for such shaping of the stuff. Even so, people who know how to observe and to draw conclusions from what they see will profit greatly. Others will be

taken in by the picture on the screen and confused
by the variety of visible things. After a while they
may even cease to feel confused: proud of their right
to see everything and weaned from the desire to
understand and to digest, they may feel great satisfaction—like those hardy British spinsters who after a
trip around the world contentedly arrive in the train
station of their home town in the same state of mind
in which they left.

The senses are useful when their contribution is not
overestimated. In the culture we happen to live in,
they teach us relatively little. The world of our century
is a poor actor: it does show its variegated outside,
but its true nature is not immediately apparent either
to the eyes or to the ears. The newsreels tell us little,
not only because the material is often badly chosen or
because we do not know how to observe. They fail
because the characteristics of the present world situation, or of a political event, or of a form of government
are not as clearly expressed in their perceivable manifestations as a man's personality may be expressed in
his face. Symptoms do not reveal much unless there is
a physician to interpret them. In order to understand
our present time, one must talk to the people, to the
industrialists, or read the memoirs of the diplomats. If
television is to make us understand the world rather
than merely showing it to us, it will, at least, have to
add the voice of the commentator to the pictures and
the music and the noises—for words can speak of the
general when we see the specific, and discuss the
causes when we are faced with the effects.

How about the asocial traits, which television in-
herits from radio? Granted that when large masses of

people see the same programs a certain unification of outlook will result. Also the exchange of programs can make for rapprochement among nations. When official pronouncements, parliamentary sessions, ceremonies, or court trials are transmitted, the citizen may feel more intimately concerned with the ways of his country. The complicated system of indirect government by which the central forces of public life reach the individual only through innumerable intermediaries is supplemented by the "wireless participation" of everybody in the affairs of state.

But doing things at the same time and doing them together is not quite the same. Radio and television do give a cozy family touch to public life, but they also keep the individual citizen from meeting his fellows. No longer does one need to be in company in order to celebrate or to mourn, to learn, to enjoy, to hail or to protest. It is true that our concert halls and theaters do not create much group feeling either. Strangers sit in rows, everyone watches and listens by himself, and the presence of the others is disturbing rather than helpful. But whenever the audience makes itself part of the event by laughing, shouting, answering, cheering, and booing, whenever the distinction between active and passive participants breaks down, something happens to the actor, the speaker, the teacher, or the preacher, as well as to the audience, the constituency, the pupils, and the congregation that cannot be replaced by electronics.

Television will make up for actual physical presence even more completely than does radio. All the more isolated will be the individual in his retreat, and the balance of trade will be correspondingly precarious:

an enormous influx of riches, consumption without services in return. The pathetic hermit, squatting in his room, hundreds of miles away from the scene that he experiences as his present life, the "viewer" who cannot even laugh or applaud without feeling ridiculous, is the final product of a century-long development, which has led from the campfire, the market place, and the arena to the lonesome consumer of spectacles today.

1938

A NEW LAOCOÖN: ARTISTIC COMPOSITES AND THE TALKING FILM

The following inquiry was suggested by a feeling of uneasiness that every talking film arouses in the author and that is not appeased by increased acquaintance with the new medium. It is a feeling that something is not right there: that we are dealing with productions which because of intrinsic contradictions of principle are incapable of true existence. Apparently the uneasiness is due to the spectator's attention being torn in two directions. In their attempts to attract the audience, two media are fighting each other instead of capturing it by united effort. Since the two media are striving to express the same matter in a twofold way, a disconcerting coincidence of two voices results, each of which is prevented by the other from telling more than half of what it would like to tell.

This practical situation called for a theoretical study of the aesthetic laws whose violation made the talking film so unsatisfactory. Such an undertaking seemed all the more urgent since I had come to suspect that the principles commonly used in discussions of the subject were wrong or at least wrongly applied. The point had been reached at which the persons concerned, at best, endeavored to interpret the nature of the new medium but had stopped asking the more basic question of whether its very existence was admissible or not. In fact, to bring up this question was considered by now offensive, defeatist, reactionary. All the more pressing seemed to me the need of trying to finally clear up the problem.

For this purpose I set out to investigate the conditions under which, quite in general, works of art can be based upon more than one medium—such as the spoken word, the image in motion, the musical sound —and what the range, nature, and value of such works might be. The result of this necessarily sketchy exploration was then applied to the talking film.

The theater successfully combines image and speech. —The two elements whose rivalry the motion picture cannot reconcile are, of course, image and speech. It is a surprising rivalry, if we remember that in daily life talk rarely keeps us from seeing, or seeing from listening. But as soon as we sit in front of the movie screen we notice such disturbances. Probably we react differently because we are not used to finding in the image of the real world the kind of formal precision that in the work of art presents—by means of the sensory data—the subject and its qualities in a clearcut, expressive way. Normally we gather from the world that surrounds us little more than vague hints, sufficient for practical orientation. Physical reality shapes and assembles things and events only in approximation of the pure, authentic "ideas" that are at the bottom of the empirical world. The imprecision of a color, the discord in a composition of lines do not necessarily interfere with our perception when we are observing for practical purposes only; and the literary impurity of a sentence may not prevent us from understanding its meaning. Therefore, when in everyday life an unbalanced combination of visual and auditory elements fails to produce discomfort, we need not be surprised either. In the realm of art, on the contrary, the unsure expression of an object, the inconsistency of a movement, a badly put phrase will impair at once the effect, the meaning, the beauty conveyed by the work. This is why a combination of media that has no unity will appear intolerable.

It seems unlikely that the union of the image in motion and the spoken word as such is the cause of the discomfort created by the "talkies"; for such compounding of the two media seems sanctioned by the theater, surely an ancient and most fruitful art. Perhaps the mistake lies in the particular way the talking film employs the time-honored combination. As a matter of fact, even the theater has been accused now and then of being basically a hybrid. Some critics have pointed out that throughout its history the theater has oscillated between two extreme procedures, which would entrust the entire production either to the visible action on the stage or to the dialogue. It may be, therefore, that the theater is trying constantly to solve an insoluble inner conflict by leaning toward one of the two purer forms of expression of which it is a mixture: the mere image in motion—as we have it in the dance—or the mere spoken word, recently used to perfection in certain radio plays. To be sure, such leaning of the theater toward the pure and extreme forms would not necessarily prove that their mixture is inadmissible. One of the most basic artistic impulses derives from man's yearning to escape the disturbing multiplicity of nature and seeks, therefore, to depict this bewildering reality with the simplest means. For this reason a medium of expression that is capable of producing complete works by its own resources will forever keep up its resistance against any combination with another medium. In the theater, then, such a tendency toward a more unified and thereby simpler medium is manifest—a tendency to attain more elementary and in a certain sense more immediately striking effects through pure visual action or pure dialogue. However, the stage director realizes also that by combining the more concrete and relatively simpler visual medium with the more abstract and complex medium of speech richer works can be produced, which may render human life more completely. For this reason he sacrifices himself to some extent—a sacrifice that often will be hard precisely on the kind of man who has the true theater blood: he imposes upon his theatrical instinct his will to function as a mere servant of the playwright's work, which he agrees to interpret, to enrich, to make more tangible. In order to succeed he must conquer his lively inclination toward the "absolute" theater, that is, the kind of performance that is sheer stage action. Such pantomime, by the way, has remained sterile whenever it was attempted and must remain so unless it be stylized to the point of becoming dance or so enriched visually as to become film.

Parallelism of complete and segregated representations.—The enrichment and unity that may result in art from the coöperation of several media are not identical with the fusion of all sorts of sense perception that is typical for our way of experiencing the "real" world. Because in art the diversity of the various perceptual media requires separations among them— separations that only a higher unity can overcome.

Obviously it would be senseless and inconceivable to try to fuse visual and auditory elements artistically in the same way in which one sentence is tied to the next, one motion to the other. For instance, the unity that exists in real life between the body and the voice of a person would be valid in a work of art only if there existed between the two components a kinship much more intrinsic than their belonging together biologically. The artist conceives and forms his image of the world through directly perceivable sensory qualities, such as colors, shapes, sounds, movements. The expressive features of these percepts serve to interpret the meaning and character of the subject. The essence of the subject must be manifest in what can be observed directly. On this (lower) level of the sensory phenomena, however, an artistic connection of visual and auditory phenomena is not possible. (One cannot put a sound in a painting!) Such a connection can be made only at a second, higher level, namely, at the level of the so-called expressive qualities. A dark red wine can have the same expression as the dark sound of a violoncello, but no formal connection can be established between the red and the sound as purely perceptual phenomena. At the second level, then, a compounding of elements that derive from disparate sensory realms becomes possible artistically.

Such compounding, however, must respect the segregations established at the lower level. It presupposes.

in fact, that in each of the sensory areas concerned a closed and complete structure has been formed on that lower plane—a structure that in its own way and by itself must present the total subject of the work of art. When at the second level the purely material barrier disappears, the elements deriving from the different areas (for instance, the visual and the auditory) must nevertheless preserve the groupings and segregations established at the primary level. On the other hand, they may take advantage of the way they resemble each other or contrast with each other as far as expression is concerned and thus create interrelationships. For instance, all the movements of a group of dancers remain unified among one another and, together, segregated from the accompanying music. Within the musical structure also all sounds are interconnected. But the similarity of the expression conveyed by the patterns of the two sensory areas makes it possible to combine them in one unitary work of art. For example, a certain gesture of one of the dancers may resemble a corresponding musical phrase with regard to expression and meaning . . . just as the gesture of an actor may correspond to the meaning of the sentence he is uttering.

The combination of several means of expression in a work of art provides us with a formal device whose particular virtue lies in that at the second structural level a relationship is established among patterns that are complete, closed, and strictly segregated at the lower or primary level. In addition to the two levels I have mentioned there may be others, higher ones— in fact, there almost always are—but they are less important. One of them concerns the characteristics of the objects represented in the work of art inasmuch as they belong to our real physical world, for example, the practical, material connections between the human body and the human voice. This level is closer to everyday life and the relations created at it are, therefore, more obvious to our common sense. But the kind of connection established at this level between patterns from different perceptual areas is not sufficient to make them homogeneous, fusable, or exchangeable. Their disparity at the primary level is in the way. For what happens at the primary level is binding for the entire work.

(It will be understood that the relationships between elements of the physical world can go beyond mere coincidence in time and space. The body and the voice of a person, for example, are not just accidental neighbors who otherwise have nothing in common. Rather, since they belong to the same organism, they are intimately related also as far as their expression goes—a similarity that makes the physical connection of that body and that voice more meaningful. But neither in art nor in reality is such empirical kinship always accompanied by a kinship of expression; nor is similarity of expression found only in things that belong together empirically.)

The objection may be raised that literature uses all the senses—sight, hearing, smell, touch, taste—liberally mixed and just as inseparably fused as we experience them in everyday life. This objection, however, can be made validly only by someone who believes that the words of the writer are nothing but a means of arousing, in the mind of the reader, memory images supposed to replace the direct perceptual sensations, which the writer cannot provide. (Thus Schopenhauer: "The simplest and correctest definition of poetry seems to me to be that poetry is the art of stimulating the power of imagination by means of words.") But is it true that literary language is nothing better than the kind of expedient to which, for instance, the writer of film scripts must resort when he wants to describe the scenes of a film to be made? Is the word only transitional or is it rather the final form of the literary creation? Does not the particular nature of literature consist precisely in the abstractness of language, which calls every object by the collective name of its species and therefore defines it only in a generic way, without reaching the object itself in its individual concreteness? It is from this particularity that literature draws its most characteristic and strongest effects. The poetical word refers directly to the meaning, the character, the structure of things; hence the spiritual quality of its vision, the acuteness and succinctness of its descriptions. The writer is not tied to the physical concreteness of a given setting; therefore, he is free to connect one object with another even though in actuality the two may not be neighbors either in time or in space. And since he uses as his material not the actual percept but its conceptual name, he can compose his images of elements that are taken from disparate sensory sources. He does not have to worry whether the combinations he creates are possible or even imaginable in the physical world. When Goethe, in one of his poems, calls the oak tree a towering giant dressed in a garment of fog, he uses of "tower" only the tallness, of "giant" only the massiveness, of "garment" only the function of covering—something no painter could do. The writer operates on what I called the second or higher level, at which the visual and auditory arts also discover their kinship. We understand now why the writer can fuse the rustling of the wind, the sailing of the clouds, the odor of rotting leaves, and the touch of raindrops on the skin into one genuine unity.

It is true that, in a different sense, the writer also reaches the level of immediate concreteness so that he, too, can profit from its animating virtues. He cannot make us see, hear, smell, or touch the things he evokes, but the words he uses to name them are sounds, that is, auditory material. The expression conveyed by the sequences of vowels and consonants, the rhythm of stresses, the legatos, and the caesuras make it possible for him to say in the different and more concrete medium of sound what at the same time he is also saying through concepts. In this sense, any literary work is in itself a composite, and thus subject to the rules we are exploring.

The conditions for the combination of artistic media. —Artistic media combine, I asserted before, as separate and complete structural forms. The theme to be expressed by a song, for instance, is given in the words of the text and again, in another manner, in the sounds of the music. Both elements conform to each other in such a way as to create the unity of the whole, but their separateness remains evident, nevertheless. Their combination resembles a successful marriage, where similarity and adaptation make for unity but where the personality of the two partners remains intact, nevertheless. It does *not* resemble the child that springs from such a marriage, in whom both components are inseparably mixed.

Similarly, in a theatrical performance the visible action and the dialogue must each present the total subject. If there is a gap in one of the two components it cannot be made up by the other. It is the duty of the director to interpret the content of the dialogue for the eyes of the audience through color, shape, and motion, through the appearance and gestures of the actors, through the spatial organization of the setting and the way the bodies move within this space. The visual performance cannot be interrupted, except if the gap serves as a delimiting interval, that is, a caesura, which does not break up the action but is a part of it. The visible action must never be permitted to become inexpressive or empty for the benefit of the dialogue because even the most substantial lines of speech could not make up for such a deficiency: they could not mend a visual gap. In the same way, an interruption of the dialogue can only take the form of an interval; it cannot be justified as a temporary shift from audible to visible action. There can be, of course, a contrapuntal opposition of a rest in the pantomime against a simultaneous exchange of heated retorts in the dialogue, or of a moment of silence against a significant piece of pantomimic action—but only in the sense in which the harmonic play of a piece of music is enriched by the frequent exits and entrances of the various voices or instruments.

The dialogue must be complete.—Enough has been said to make it clear that there is little justification for a current fad on the part of some "highbrow" film directors who have the action carried almost entirely by the visual performance on the screen and only here and there add a touch of dialogue to the dramatic development. Such a procedure evidently does not create a parallelism between two complete components, namely, a very dense visual part and a very "porous" auditory one: instead the dialogue is fragmentary; it consists of pieces that are separated by unbridgeable interruptions. The expressed intention of these directors is to have speech emerge, in certain highspots, as a kind of condensation of the visual image. The distinction of the media is entirely neglected, and as a result scraps of speech pop up with a ludicrous surprise effect, out of empty auditory space, in which they float without anchor. The defect cannot be eliminated by filling the stretches of silence with appropriate noises or music; for the example of the song has taught us already that even within the realm of auditory art, music and speech can be combined only when a parallelism between two complete and segregated components—a poem and a melody— is provided. If the dialogue were not dispersed in pieces but collected in large complexes, each of which were a closed and continuous structure, one could at least refer to the great example of Beethoven's *Ninth Symphony*, and the later similar attempt by Mahler, in which at the climax of the composition the instrumental music is completed by human voices so that from that moment on the work proceeds on a broader, more monumental base. However, in the talking film even that device would not help because there still would remain the obstacle of the difference in visual style between the silent scenes and those completed with dialogue.

The practical experience of what goes on in the movie theater would demonstrate to everybody that a true fusion of word and image is impossible if the image on the screen were ever shut off so that the dialogue could try to "take over." The visual action is always complete—at least technically, although not artistically. The complete visual action accompanied by occasional dialogue represents a partial parallelism, not a fusion. The fragmentary nature of the dialogue is the fundamental defect. (To be sure, an interruption of the dialogue does not produce the same kind of psychological shock that would result from a sudden disappearance of the image from the screen. The reason is that, psychologically, a stop of the dialogue is not perceived as an interruption of the auditory action, the way the disappearance of the image from the screen would interrupt the visual performance. Silence is not necessarily experienced as the removal of the world of sound but rather as a neutral foil—empty but "positive," as the plain background of a portrait is a part of the picture. However, a phenomenon may not disturb us in a purely psychological sense and still be objectionable artistically.)

Those patches of speech are of little theoretical importance as long as they represent merely the minimum concession of a film director who has to meet the demands for dialogue on the part of producers and distributors. For in that case the film maker thinks of his work as a silent film, that is, as a film in the true meaning of the term, adulterated by a hostile principle (that imposes the talking upon the artist). If, however, he believes that simply by reducing the amount of speech and thus moving away from the style of the theater he approaches a new and autonomous art form, namely, the "talking film," he demonstrates his lack of professional sensibility. The fewer words are used and the more definitely the burden of the action is carried by the image on the screen, the more disturbing, alien, and ridiculous will the speech fragments appear; it will be all the more evident that what is being used is the traditional style of the silent film—but in an impure fashion.

In comparison, the approach of the more modest craftsmen who work in the studios at the service of the film industry is artistically saner. By their daily contact with their medium they have attained some intuitive understanding of its intrinsic requirements, and for that reason—at least partly—they tend toward the "100 per cent dialogue" film. In these productions, speech accompanies the film throughout its length, more or less without gaps, and in that way fulfills one of the elementary conditions for the compounding of media, namely, parallelism. In the average film of that kind one notices, in addition, an ever more radical curtailment of the means of visual expression as they were developed during the period of the silent movies. This tendency also derives, as I am going to show, from the aesthetic conditions created by the talking film. Even so, the disequilibrium between image and speech is not avoided by this procedure nor does it create artistically valid sound films. Instead, the studio practice moves toward the traditional style of the theater without being ready to renounce the novel charms of the moving picture.

In any case, complete dialogue would be the basic premise for any use of speech in film—an artistically complete and closed word pattern. We need to inquire now whether or not this condition can be met by a technique that would be different in principle from that of the theater.

Can image and word be combined in a manner different from that of the theater?—The specialty of such a new art form might be based on some fundamental difference between theater action and film action, as far as the visual part of the performance is concerned. Commonly it is taken for granted that such a difference does exist and is demonstrated by actual practice. And yet there is no fundamental reason why the distinguishing traits of the film image should be denied to the theater. Unquestionably, the theater as an art form would remain essentially what it is if the flesh-and-blood actor were replaced with his photographic image: the theater performances on television prove it. The theater also could substitute black-and-white for natural color—and, of course, monochrome is no essential characteristic of the movies anyway. The displacement of the entire picture, as produced by traveling shots in film, has recently been obtained also in the theater through rotating stages and similar devices—more modestly, to be sure, but matters of degree count little for distinctions in principle. The modern theater has also used actual film projections, for instance, as backdrops. Granted that in its present form the theater cannot change the distance or the angle of view, nor can it leap from place to place as the film does by means of montage. But here again we merely need to think of television in order to realize that what is technically impossible for the theater as we know it today may be familiar tomorrow.

In this connection we might as well realize that film is art, yes, but not an entirely new and isolated art. The art of the moving image is distinct from that of the static image, as we have it in painting or sculpture. However, it comprises not only the film but also dance and pantomime; and the question is at least debatable whether or not the properties that film derives from the technique of mechanical registration are weightier than the others it shares with dance, pantomime, and therefore also with the theater. One thing seems certain: if one tries to ignore the properties that the film shares with other media—as has been done *ad majorem gloriam* of the movies—one cannot hope correctly to evaluate the art of the film. The art of the moving image is as old as the other arts, it is as old as humanity itself, and the motion picture is but its most recent manifestation. What is more, I would venture to predict that the film will be able to reach the heights of the other arts only when it frees itself from the bonds of photographic reproduction and becomes a pure work of man, namely, as animated cartoon or painting.

There is, then, no difference in principle between the visual action of the theater and the moving image of the film. Therefore, the experiences made with the "enriched image" in the theater can be directly applied to the talking film. What are these experiences? They show that attempts at "enrichment" have quickly turned out to be deviations from serious stage art. When the designer indulges in dazzling contrivances and the director crowds the stage with action, the visual performance distracts from the words of the playwright rather than interprets them.

Of course, this contention presupposes that the stage performance has the purpose of providing the dialogue with its due position in the foreground while leaving to the image only a secondary, supporting function. We need now to explore the possibility of other artistic forms that might do without this presupposition.

The simpler the wording of the dialogue, the less likely the audience will be kept from following the dramatic conversation attentively. Now a work of dramatic literature, just as any other work of art, can assume any degree of density—from the intricate and heavy thought of a Shakespeare, who presents our receptive powers with almost insoluble tasks even when there is nothing visual at all to distract us from the recital (as, for example, in radio performances), to the loosest lines of plainest concreteness. The simpler forms of dialogue—which might not be less valuable literarily—could receive a richer visual presentation without suffering from it. Perhaps the history of literature offers few examples of such simple dialogue, but conceivably this could change if the playwright got used to the idea of seeing his works completed by a richer stage action. In fact, perhaps the writer himself might undertake the task of working in both media, that is, of creating by himself the twofold total work. Let us assume this happened and the scales tipped gradually in favor of the visual action: we should then arrive first at works in which the audible and the visible were in balance, and finally at others in which the picture predominated whereas the dialogue would accept a secondary function, similar to that reserved nowadays for the pantomimic action on the theater stage.

Would productions of this latter kind belong to a new and autochthonous species of art? Could a mere quantitative shift of the components give birth to a new art form? The performance of a large group of dancers may be accompanied by nothing but one flute or, conversely, the solo of one dancer may be accompanied by a whole symphony orchestra . . . are we dealing with different art forms? There would be no particular hurry in deciding whether we were faced with a mere variety of theater art or rather with a special form all of its own—if only the indicated shift of elements would give us new ways of representing our life, new ways of saying things for which so far there is no tongue. All depends now on deciding whether or not the procedure that we have drawn up in theory is capable of life in practice.

Specific characteristics of various artistic media.— Earlier I explained that the compounding of different media—for example, moving picture and speech— cannot be justified simply by the fact that in the experience of everyday life visual and auditory elements are intimately connected and, in fact, inseparably fused. There must be artistic reasons for such a combination: it must serve to express something that could not be said by one of the media alone. We found that a composite work of art is possible only if complete structures, produced by the media, are integrated in the form of parallelism. Naturally, such a "double track" will make sense only if the components do not simply convey the same thing. They must complete each other in the sense of dealing differently with the same subject. Each medium must treat the subject in its own way, and the resulting differences must be in accordance with those that exist between the media.

That the various media are different in character has been shown in Lessing's *Laocoön* by the example of the visual arts and literature. In distinguishing, for example, between representational and nonrepresentational media one understands easily that painting or the dance—as contrasted with music—may convey underlying themes in a more indirect and hidden manner. The representation is tied to tangible objects but precisely for this reason more in keeping with practical experience. Music transmits such ideas more directly, more purely and forcefully, but its interpretation, which can do without depicting objects, is also more abstract and generic since it excludes the multitude of concrete things and happenings. This is why music completes the dance and the silent film so perfectly: it vigorously transmits the feelings and moods and also the inherent rhythm of movements that the visual performance would wish to describe but which are accessible to it only through the inevitable diffraction and turbidity deriving from the use of concrete objects.

There is no point in comparing the relative value of the various media. Personal preferences exist, but each medium reaches the heights in its own way. If we call literature the most complete medium of all, we have to remember, nevertheless, that this universality makes also for weaknesses, where other media show particular strength. But as far as content goes, the word has the range of all the other media together: it can describe the things of this world as immobile or as constantly changing; with inimitable ease it can leap from one place to the other, from one moment to the next; it presents not only the world of our outer senses but also the entire realm of the soul, the imagination, the emotion, the will. And not only does the word capture these external and internal facts in themselves —it also includes the logical and the intuitive connections that the human mind establishes between them. It can present objects at almost any degree of abstractness: from individual concreteness to rarefied generality. It can swing back and forth between percept and concept and thereby satisfy the most earthly as well as the most spiritual demands. And particularly it is at home on the attractive meeting ground of phenomenon and idea, where the poet operates.

Visual action as a useful complement of the dramatic dialogue.—Even so, at the one extreme of the scale that leads from percept to concept, language cannot go beyond a certain degree of approximation. It cannot materialize things to the point of presenting us with their material nature itself. It can say "color" but cannot show us color. Hence the practice of completing the spoken dialogue with stage action and stories with illustrations. At the same time we understand that such a completion is not necessary. The writer can describe to us any object with the degree of precision required for his artistic purpose.

A play, therefore, does not require staging—it merely permits it. Accordingly, the sets as well as the motions of the actors should humbly yield the limelight to the dramatic work, which is complete in itself. The production comes into being only after the poet has finished his work, freely and without much consideration. The stage action gives body to the indirect vision conveyed by the poet. Colors, shapes, and noises serve the simpler and more elementary experience of the senses, which is welcome to the audience and to which the poet himself pays tribute with the sound and rhythm of his words. Sound and image are primordial art, closer to nature than the rendering by concepts. Music, painting, sculpture, architecture, dance, and film appeal to the more primitive side of the human mind. Although enlightened by speech, man nevertheless cherishes these ancient resources and their vigorously simple interpretation of what he has to say.

Being more concrete and biologically older, the image can produce the more massive effects, so that the word is threatened when the picture, and particularly the moving picture, presents itself. A good stage production endeavors to tone down the natural dominance of the visible performance by keeping it at a certain distance from the audience and by restricting the amount of action on the stage.

Could not the visual action become an integral part of the play?—In the theater, the visual action is, then, a servant of the dialogue. On the other hand, it does not simply repeat what the playwright says or could say. By presenting the subject in a particular way, which is not accessible to literature, the visual action satisfies one of the conditions for the combination of media. This being so, is it not conceivable that in certain cases language might seem an insufficient instrument for the artist who creates for the theater?

Are there not things he could not express in words but only through stage action? So that he might find it necessary to use both media?

Playwrights include in their plays references to the external stage action to varying degrees. There is, on the one hand, the kind of poet who concentrates entirely on internal action. All he wishes to present is the clash of psychical forces, expressed in the words of the dialogue. Probably there are few actual examples of this extreme case, although the radio play tends to develop in this direction. At the opposite pole we find a kind of play that might consist of nothing but external action—which would change the playwright into a narrator of pantomime.

There are, of course, two ways by which the writer may put in his play necessary references to external action. The classical procedure of the great dramatists is that of including them in the dialogue itself. In addition, we find, generally, also stage directions, which describe the setting and what is going on in it. Directions may be rare and short, as in the classics, or—as in some modern plays—they may grow into lengthy descriptions of the type found in novels. However, they do not necessarily have to be considered as a second medium. We are not dealing here with an invasion of visual action into playwriting but rather with the adoption of techniques of fiction. There is a recognizable difference between the literary description of visual action and attempts to describe in words something to be produced visually. In the latter case, as we know from the technique of the film scriptwriter, words are used as a mere expedient. When a poet describes a painting, the result is not a painting, and is not intended to be one. On the other hand, an attempt to fixate with words a piece of visual action, simply because no other means of recording is available, will easily turn out to be absurd literarily and to make excessive demands on the visual imagination of the reader, even though the description may come from a gifted writer. As an example I will translate a piece by the eighteenth-century writer G. Ch. Lichtenberg, who tried to preserve in words the great Garrick's interpretation of the scene in which Hamlet sees the ghost of his father. "Garrick turns suddenly around and at the same moment falls two or three steps backward with his knees apart; his hat drops to the floor; both of his arms, and particularly the left, are raised, the left hand is at the height of the head, the right arm is more bent, the right hand lower, the fingers are spread out and the mouth is open; thus he stops, as though paralyzed, in the midst of a large but not excessive step, supported by his friends, who are more familiar with the apparition and fear he may collapse; in his face, horror is expressed in such a way that it made me shiver even before he began to speak."

If, then, there is a genuine difference between the literary description of visual matter and the recording in words of things belonging in a nonliterary, visual medium, is it not possible that a writer may find it necessary to have his dramatic dialogue completed by—not just accompanied with—a specific kind of visual staging? This indeed would be a basically new type of art, as shown also by the fact that the author himself would have to take care in detail of the visual production since it would represent "the other half" of his work itself rather than simply a subsequent "performance" of it.

So far, artists have preferred the singular medium.— The great artists, whose activity represents, as it were, the practical manifestation of the aesthetic laws, have shown little inclination thus far to make use of such a possibility. Shakespeare lived in daily contact with the world of the theater, but Goethe could say of him, nevertheless, that he was not a theater writer and did not think of the theater when he wrote. There is, in fact, no more radical way than his of anticipating every possible stage effect and, therefore, to make an adequate stage performance in our sense impossible. Similarly, the plays of Molière, Goethe, Schiller, Goldoni—all theater people—are complete even on paper, and the same is true for the Greek classics. Certain plays, in which the descriptions of the setting, the characters, and the action make up a considerable part of the text—for example. *A Midsummer Night's Dream,* or Kleist's *Penthesilea*—seem practically un-stageable because the poet's words create images so powerful and phantastic that it may be considered ridiculous to try to match them or even improve on them in the production.

In the entire recorded history of art we find only one example of some weight that involves not just the secondary addition of one medium to the other but, to some extent, the collective effort of two media, namely, the opera. If we examine it, however, we find that in practice one of the components, the musical, dominates decisively. In fact, the libretto is a mere vehicle for the purposes of the music. Often it is put together strictly according to the needs of the composer, and its literary value tends to be slight. It is not essential for the true substance of the opera and serves mainly to explain the plot and to make a stage production possible. (The work of Richard Wagner approaches an equilibrium of music and libretto, but this work is so debatable and so strongly influenced by theory that by itself it does not represent a valid counterargument.) In fact, historically, the coming about of the opera probably represents not so much a union of music and literature but the conquest of the dramatic element on the part of music, which is otherwise limited to the lyrical style. Generated by the attempts of the fifteenth century to enhance, through music, the dramatic and spectacular qualities of the tragedies in the Greek manner, it actually satisfies the wish to express musically the strivings and emotions of man in action and the situations of conflict or harmony that arise from social intercourse. Dialogue is used as a technical and secondary means to make the human actor audible in the most natural way and to develop the plot beyond those elementary themes that can be made comprehensible by the moving image of pantomime plus music alone. In other words, the opera is an almost entirely musical form, and the dialogue is limited more or less to the task of the printed "titles" in silent movies.

It is worth remembering here also that great actors often prefer mediocre plays that allow them to work almost by improvisation and thus to reserve the performance essentially to the expression of body and voice; whereas, on the other hand, their genius often spells danger to the great works of dramatic literature.

Similarly, good dancers and the makers of silent films have a preference for simple, clear-cut music, which may not be first-rate.

All these facts taken together suggest that up to now artists have shown little capacity or inclination to produce works genuinely based on more than one medium. To be sure, in all the examples cited more than one medium is actually used, but as a rule a different person takes care of each medium, and one of them assumes the lead: the dominant medium develops a rich structure from the theme sustained more simply by the secondary medium. Not that the secondary medium should ever be neglected to the point of being cheap, or smothered to the extent of being unable to make its point. Art admits a hierarchy of function but does not tolerate the qualitative or quantitative atrophy of any component, once it is included.

The hierarchy of media in the work of art.—In composite works, the various media—as well as the artists who take care of them—seem to form hierarchies. The dramatic productions of antiquity illustrate this best. In them the word of the poet dominates, but it is complemented by stage action, which broadly outlines the dramatic events, and also by music. Another example may be found in the medieval cathedral, where the architectonic structure is enriched by painting and sculpture. Add to this the presence and participation of the theater audience and the religious congregation, and you have art as an all-embracing ritual rather than as the isolated object it becomes at a late stage of civilization. These hierarchic productions tend to be, as we pointed out, the work not of one but of several persons, and in order truly to succeed such a

collaboration is likely to presuppose a spiritual com-
munity, that is, in the more general sense: the existence
of a cult. The individual artist, on the other hand, tends
to conceive the world in one medium only.

The coöperation of several artists helps to overcome
the discrepancy of the different perceptual media.
Each artist can limit himself to one sensory universe.
The total product may turn out to be incoherent, of
course, particularly when no medium takes the lead
decisively and instead there is an approximate equilibrium of two or more of them. This happens, for
instance, in certain songs. Like the opera, the song is
an essentially musical form. But when the poem that
has been set to music succeeds in attracting considerable attention in its own right, the balance between
music and poetry seems unstable. Such a rivalry among
the media may keep the listener from making real
contact with the work: he may not get beyond enjoy-
ing the rather formalistic fascination deriving from
the consonance of similar yet heterogeneous components.

Possible advantages of the film dialogue.—We have
now worked out some fundamental concepts, which
can be useful in judging the talking film. From what
I have said it follows that, first of all, there should
be a dominant medium. This part would fall to the
moving image since predominance of the word would
lead to the theater. The question is, then, whether
the art of the animated image, which has been developed as the silent film, could use the kind of libretto
through which the opera provides a skeleton of the
dramatic action.

First of all, we must repeat here that by means of

the opera libretto (as well as its predecessors in church music, etc.) music conquered a vast new realm, namely, that of dramatic music or the musical drama. In the case of the film, the dialogue does not give access to a new type of work. At best, it enlarges what exists. We have to remember that in silent film the, dialogue, as given in the titles, was not at all the foundation and starting point of the work, from which the pictures were developed. They were a mere expedient added secondarily and for the purpose of explanation to works conceived and realized in images. Perhaps the spoken dialogue may not be able to fulfill even this humble function. What is useful for the opera, may be harmful for the film.

Will an artist, that is, a person guided by a sure sensitivity for the medium he employs, ever feel impelled to "set" a dialogue "to pictures" instead of creating in pictures? Since pictures are what attract him, he might be tempted by speech as a technical device that would sharpen the meaning of his scenes, save him the tortuous detours necessary to explain the plot, and open up a larger field of subjects. Now, in fact, dialogue makes possible an extensive development of the external action, and particularly also the internal action. No fairly complicated event or state of mind can be conveyed by pictures alone. Therefore, the addition of spoken dialogue has made storytelling easier. In this sense, film dialogue has been defined by some critics as a device for saving time, space, and ingenuity—a saving that would reserve the available limited length of the film and the creative energy of the maker for the truly relevant content of the work. It remains to be seen, however, whether there is, in the movies, any justification for the kind of involved plot that we find in the novel and the play.

We can easily understand why the large movie audience has applauded the introduction of the spoken word. What the audience wants is to take part in exciting events as fully as possible. The best way of achieving this is, in a certain sense, the mixture of visual action and dialogue: external events are shown concretely to the eye, and at the same time the thoughts, intentions, and emotions of the characters are communicated through words in the directest and most natural way. Moreover the felt presence of the events is enormously enhanced by the sound of voices and other noises. The audience will object only when the dialogue is cut down so much that it does not explain the action or when, on the contrary, there is too little outer action, and all the talking becomes tiresome. In a crude way, these objections to the talking film are the same as those of the connoisseur.

Dialogue narrows the world of the film.—The example of the opera seemed to justify and recommend the use of dialogue. But not without caution can we compare the art of sound and the art of pictures in their relation to the spoken word. One of the main characteristics of dramatic dialogue is that it limits the action to the human performer. This suits music perfectly since, as we said, the opera was created precisely in order to represent human beings in dramatic action musically. The image, of course, does not need dialogue to present man, but in the visual world the human kind does not enjoy the leading role it has on the stage. Granted that in certain paintings human figures hold the foreground gigantically; but just as often painting shows man as a part of his environment, which gives meaning to him and to which he gives meaning. Man appears as a part of the Creation, from which he can be isolated only artificially. The moving picture was from the beginning more concerned with the world animated by man than with man set off against his world. Therefore, to be limited by dialogue to the performances of the human figure was bound to seem intolerable.

The presentation of man's natural setting had been one of the achievements that justified the existence of the movies next to the theater. Naturally, the silent film also had often shown the actor in close-ups. But more importantly, it had created a union of silent man and silent things as well as of the (audible) person close-by and the (inaudible) one at a far distance. In the universal silence of the image, the fragments of a broken vase could "talk" exactly the way a character talked to his neighbor, and a person approaching on a road and visible on the horizon as a mere dot "talked" as someone acting in close-up. This homogeneity, which is completely foreign to the theater but familiar to painting, is destroyed by the talking film: it endows the actor with speech, and since only he can have it, all other things are pushed into the background.

Now there is a limit to the visual expression that can be drawn from the human figure, particularly if the picture has to accompany dialogue. Pure pantomime knows of three ways to overcome this limitation. It can give up the portraying of plots and instead present the "absolute" movement of the body, that is, dance. Here the human body becomes an instrument for melodic and harmonic forms, which are superior to mere pantomime, as music is superior to a (hypothetical) art of natural noises. Secondly, pantomime can adopt the solution of the silent film, namely, become a part of the richer universe in motion. And finally, it can become subservient to dramatic speech—as it does in the theater. But to the pantomime of the talking film all three of these solutions are inaccessible: it cannot become dance because dance does not need speech and perhaps does not even tolerate it; it cannot submerge in the huge *orbis pictus* of the silent film because of its tie to the human figure; and it cannot become the servant of speech without giving up its own self.

The dialogue paralyzes visual action.—Not only does speech limit the motion picture to an art of dramatic portraiture, it also interferes with the expression of the image. The better the silent film, the more strictly it used to avoid showing people in the act of talking, important though talking is in real life. The actors expressed themselves by posture and facial expression. Additional meaning came from the way the figure was shown within the framework of the picture, by lighting, and particularly by the total context of sequence and plot. The visual counterpart of speech, that is, the monotonous motions of the mouth, yields little and, in fact, can only hamper the expressive movement of the body. The motions of the mouth convincingly demonstrate that the activity of talking compels the actor into visually monotonous, meaningless, and often ludicrous behavior.

It is obvious that speech cannot be attached to the immobile image (painting, photography); but it is equally ill-suited for the silent film, whose means of expression resemble those of painting. It was precisely the absence of speech that made the silent film develop a style of its own, capable of condensing the dramatic situation. To separate or to find each other, to win or to give in, to be friends or enemies—all such themes were neatly presented by a few simple attitudes, such as a raising of the head or of an arm, or the bowing of one person to another. This had led to a most cine-genic species of tale, which was full of simple happenings and which, with the coming of the talking film, was replaced by a theater-type play, poor in external action but well developed psychologically. This meant replacing the visually fruitful image of man in action with the sterile one of the man who talks.

As far as the opera is concerned, there is no objection to the dialogue centering the action around the human character; nor is there any to the visual paralysis of the actor. What the opera wants is, we said, the musical expression of man in action. It has little use for the expressive virtues of the animated image on the stage, which remains secondary, complementary, explicatory. The opera director does not hesitate to stop the stage action in favor of long arias. This gives the dialogue plenty of time, and in fact too much time: phrases have to be stretched and repeated to comply with the music. So that what hurts the film does not hurt the opera.

If after discussing the theoretical difficulties that lie in the way of the talking film we look around to see whether in practice the motion-picture production has worked out satisfactory solutions, we find our diagnosis confirmed. The average talking film today endeavors to combine visually poor scenes full of dialogue with the completely different traditional style of rich, silent action. In comparison with the epoch of the silent film there is also an impressive decline of artistic excellence, in the average films as well as in the peak productions—a trend that cannot be due entirely to the ever increasing industrialization.

It may seem surprising that mankind should produce in large number works based on a principle that represents such a radical artistic impoverishment if compared with the available purer forms. But is such a contradiction really surprising at a time at which in other respects, too, so many people live a life of unreality and fail to attain the true nature of man and its fitting manifestations? If the opposite happened in the movies, would not such a pleasant inconsistency be even more surprising?

There is comfort, however, in the fact that hybrid forms are quite unstable. They tend to change from their own unreality into purer forms, even though this may mean a return to the past. Beyond our blundering there are inherent forces that, in the long run, overcome error and incompleteness and direct human action toward the purity of goodness and truth.